COMMUNITY AND DISUNITY:

SYMBOLS OF GRACE AND SIN

by
Jerome P. Theisen, O.S.B.

Preface by
Piet Schoonenberg, S.J.

ST. JOHN'S UNIVERSITY PRESS
Collegeville, Minnesota
1985

Cover by Placid Stuckenschneider, O.S.B.

Library of Congress Cataloging in Publication Data

Theisen, Jerome P., 1930-
  Community and disunity.

  Bibliography: p.
  1. Sin. 2. Christian communities. I. Title.
BT715.T45 1985   241'.3   84-27580
ISBN 0-8146-1406-X

Table of Contents

Preface

Abbot Jerome Theisen asked me to write a preface for this book and I am eager to do so. What motivates me is not only the hospitality of Saint John's Abbey which I enjoyed several times, and not only the opportunity to teach three summer courses at Saint John's, one in collaboration with Abbot Jerome. It is the book itself which evokes my interest, especially since it treats a matter which I have researched and about which I published a long time ago.

The present book, however, is the fruit of the author's study of many other and more recent publications in the fields of theological reflection on Scripture and Christian tradition as well as of psychology, sociology, and philosophy. The presence of moral evil, which in its relation to God is called sin, urges us to question its origin. What is it in us that enables and invites us to sin, even prior to an historical fall, even in the biblical paradise itself, to the surprise of those theologians who used to speculate on an "original justice"? And what accounts for the chain of sin in our history and for our communion and complicity in sin? Abbot Jerome, in the first chapter of his book, presents us a clear survey of old and recent answers given to these two questions, answers that vary and converge at the same time.

But the main purpose of this book is to describe sin in its own being (or non-being), to re-think the Christian and other reflections on sin, to "re-symbolize" it according to our contemporary understanding. The second chapter, therefore, describes sin under the symbol of *dis-unity*. Disunity is more than multiplicity; it is the refusal of unity on all levels. Unity, on the contrary, as *community*, is the fruit and hence the symbol of grace, and as such is described in the third and final chapter. Ultimately it is the fellowship in Christ, a fellowship which, in the sinful situation of all of us, is a community of forgiveness, founded in the saving life and death of our Lord Jesus Christ. Such a fellowship is the aim of a monastic community which Abbot Jerome can describe out of his own experience as a member and as leader of Saint John's Abbey.

After all, the idea developed in the third chapter is the leading principle of the whole book, so that, in the title, the words Community and Grace rightly precede that of Disunity and Sin. God is *our* Father, the God of community. The presence of this God is either accepted as grace or refused in sin. This message is elaborated not in theoretical reflection but in very practical suggestions. It calls for an examination of conscience about the good we contribute to the Christian and human community, the evil we inflict upon it, and last but not least, the good we fail to do. Such an examination, however, is not simply a moral analysis of our our behavior, as is fitting to the Stoa. The book invites us to reflect on the ways we experience God's call to community in Christ and respond to it. May it be read this way.

Piet Schoonenberg, S.J.

Introduction

The question of evil has exercised the minds of humans as far back as we have historical records. Why is there evil in the world? Why do disasters happen? Why do people fail each other and themselves?

In this study I do not intend to deal with all aspects of the question of evil but only some of those that pertain to moral evil: the deliberate and willful choosing of evil on the part of humans. More specifically I wish to examine some of the preconditions of moral evil, those structures of human existence that predispose a person for the pursuit of moral evil. Many forces are brought to bear on persons as they make their way through a life of human existence. The forces are many but surely they include structures that stem from biological evolution, from involvement in society, from the dynamics of the human psyche, and from the laws of economics. And ultimately the forces emerge from the depths of human volition.

This study points up the many contrary forces that come to play in the conduct of human life. They will be articulated under the verbal symbol of "disunity." The symbol of disunity seems to be basic in the description of the actual conditions of human life; it both articulates a condition and provides some understanding of the reasons for moral failure which is called sin.

One of the reasons for undertaking this study is to search for new ways of articulating a theology of sin, in particular a theology of original sin. The traditional doctrine of original sin has always been difficult to understand and even more difficult to believe. Many features of the traditional doctrine of original sin are no longer acceptable; that is, they are not found to be in contact with the word of the Gospel or the thrust of the decrees of Church councils. The doctrine needs re-interpretation today, and in fact it has received much attention in the past few decades. The purpose of this study is to examine the human condition of sin and to suggest a symbol, that of disunity, to articulate theologically the estrangement dimension of human existence. Original sin may well be the all-pervasive disunity that we experience in the conduct of our human life. It is a disunity that finds its deepest level in self-centered distance from the God of the universe, but it is a disunity that pervades human life in all its connections and dimensions.

While the major portion of the study is directed to the examination of the predispositions and the condition of sin (Chapters 1 and 2), I do not wish to leave the impression that disunity is the basic dimension of human existence. A condition of disunity affects all aspects of our life, but it is not the main feature of our existence.

There is another and more important aspect to our Christian and human life on this planet. It is the aspect of community. Just as no one escapes the condition of disunity, so everybody who comes into the world lives his or her life in the context of community. While disunity is the condition of evil, community is the condition of good. In the final analysis community is the symbol of grace. The divine favor that we call grace is ultimately directed to the formation of a community: a community of peoples on this earth, a community of believers in Jesus Christ, a community of the dead and newly alive in the presence of the loving God. Community is the ultimate favor of God. Theologically the word community functions as a verbal symbol of the goal of all divine giving and human striving. Thus, I wish to provide in Chapter 3 a short theology of community in order to identify the goal of human strivings, the goal that overcomes the condition of disunity and that constitutes the perfection of human living.

I wish to thank the many people who provided time and encouragement for this study. Saint John's Abbey and University granted me a sabbatical in 1978-79 to pursue this study. The University of Chicago's School of Divinity granted me a fellowship and a locus for this study. I am particularly indebted to Professors Paul Ricoeur and David Tracy for their lectures and counsel. I am also appreciative of my students who heard portions of this study and who provided important comments. I wish to thank my colleague, Father Joseph Kremer, for reading the manuscript and giving me valuable suggestions. I express my gratitude to Mrs. Elaine Vogel for patiently and accurately typing various drafts of this study. I am grateful to my confrere, Brother James Zarr, O.S.B., for skillfully editing the manuscript. Finally, I am indebted to Mrs. Charlotte Butcher and Mr. Alfred G. Muellerleile for financial assistance in the publication of this book.

Chapter 1

Sin: Attempts to Explain Its Origin

Moral failure is a puzzling fact of life. Many persons agree that there is sin in the world, that moral failure marks human existence. Not everyone, to be sure, acknowledges the presence of sin, but Christians characteristically view sin and its forgiveness as basic realities of human life, realities, in fact, that require divine revelation for their adequate understanding. Sin and forgiveness are the backdrop for any knowledge of redemption in Christ.

But can one proceed beyond the statement that moral failure is a puzzling fact of life? Can one reasonably search for causes of sin? Or does the search itself betray an unworthy aim: the presumption that one is seeking a scapegoat? At times this is surely the case. The story of Genesis suggests such a search for an excuse: "The search for a cause is itself the search for a scapegoat, as Adam blames Eve, Eve blames the serpent, the serpent could have blamed Lucifer, and Lucifer could have blamed the temptations implicit in the idea of Order . . . ."[1] It is possible to search for a scapegoat in order to excuse oneself from sin.[2] It is also possible, however, to acknowledge sin in one's heart and still look for causes or reasons for sin beyond one's own twisted willfulness. In the following pages both the human heart and the world beyond the heart will be examined for the reasons of moral failure, or more accurately, for the *conditions* of moral failure. It is assumed here that the theological search for the origin of sin is still valid, even though no final clarity can be assured.

1. An Historical Fall

An historical fall has long stood as an explanation of the origin of sin. Original sin was the accepted symbol of the beginning of sin. The theology of original sin focused on the disobedience of Adam and Eve as the historical beginning and cause of sin in the world. It was assumed generally that the creation of the universe itself took place only a few thousand years before Christ, that Adam and Eve lived briefly in paradise, that they sinned by disobeying an explicit command of God, that they lost his friendship and preternatural gifts, and that they began to experience a harsh and difficult existence on the face of the earth. The Adamic myth "tends to concentrate all the evil of history in a single man, in a single act—in short, in a unique event."[3]

Original sin was a theological way of expressing the idea that a fault occurred at the historical beginning of human life on the earth. The sin affected, not just the original couple, but also their posterity, all peoples of the earth. Children were born subsequently without the marvelous gifts of divine intimacy and human excellence. They were shorn of the paradisiacal privileges and had to wander the earth burdened with fumbling ignorance and unruly passions. They were subject to poignant suffering and cruel death. They bore a tradition of sin, a sinful condition that affected everyone from age to age.

The posterity of Adam and Eve had to wait in patience and sorrow for the saving hand of God; he alone could lift them once more to the level of his favor. Humankind was completely powerless to hasten the day of God's healing hand; the sons and daughters of the original couple could only wait for the renewal of God's benefactions.

Original sin was historical. It happened in the beginning of human existence but its consequences affected everyone that appeared on the face of the earth. It was an historical fall that brought its power to bear on subsequent ages. To explain the present conditions of sin, suffering, lust, and death, it was enough to cite the historical sin of long ago. Original sin as a theological symbol was the shorthand expression of the historical fall and its divine and human effects.

Today it is clear, at least to a great number of Christians, that this understanding of the Genesis story is too literal and that a nonliteral interpretation of the first chapters of Genesis contains important truths about the human condition of sin without demanding a paradise in the beginning and the devastating consequences of an historically first sin.[4] There is indeed a history of sin, one that goes back to the origin of humans on this planet. There are indeed the historical sins of individuals that influence other members of the human community. But it is denied generally that one sin of an original couple brought the huge avalanche of sin upon humankind.

2. God and the Demonic

Since God is the creative principle of the whole universe, it seems to follow that he is the direct cause of all being, both good and evil. It seems logical to assume that he is equally the source of good and evil, since nothing happens in the universe without his sustaining power.

Christian doctrine, however, opposes this radical solution to the question of evil. In keeping with a teaching that has its roots in the Hebrew Scriptures, Christian thought proclaims the goodness of all creation. The ancient Hebrews insisted that the one God is the Creator of all that exists, that the supposition of a second or third god of evil must be rejected. The first chapter of Genesis forcefully enunciates the uniqueness of the creating God. The book was written in a milieu where it was common to ascribe evil to gods. In the Babylonian creation myth *Enuma Elish* two principles of evil antedate the creation of humans: the primordial chaos and the conflict between the gods. Humans stem from evil; they are created from the blood of the murdered god Kingu who incited Tiamat to attack the gods. Human beings, in this myth, are created for menial toil; they replace the gods who were so engaged. Humans, therefore, discover the presence of pre-existing evil and at the same time they continue it.[5] By way of contrast, the Hebrew Scriptures acknowledge the presence of evil in the world, but they do not proclaim a second god of evil.

There are Hebrew texts, it is true, which ascribe evil directly to God. The Exodus account of the Egyptian plagues relates that the Lord God hardened Pharaoh's heart: "But the Lord made Pharaoh obstinate, and he would not listen to them, just as the Lord had foretold to Moses" (Exod 9:12. Cf. 7:3; 10:1, 20, 27). Other passages in the story indicate that Pharaoh hardened his own heart (Exod 8:15,28; 9:34). The point seems to be that God effects his will and his signs through the agency of both Moses and Pharaoh; the authors of the account are interested in what God is doing for his people, not in the intricacies of freedom and determinism or in a possible divine cause of evil.[6]

In the First Book of Kings, too, it is narrated that the Lord put a lying spirit in the mouths of the prophets of Ahab (1 Kgs 22:19-23; cf. 2 Chr 18:18-22). But here also the biblical author is not concerned about the cause of evil. He intends to show the overarching plan and power of God, namely that the divine designs are universally effective.[7]

A similar idea is found among the prophets. While Ezekiel forcefully proclaims the personal responsibility of each Israelite, he also speaks in terms of God's beguiling of prophets. On the one hand, Ezekiel says that God beguiles the prophet that is consulted by an idolator: "As for the prophet, if he is beguiled into speaking a word, I, the Lord, shall have beguiled that prophet; I will stretch out my hand against him and root him out of my people Israel" (Ezek 14:9). On the other hand, speaking in the name of God, Ezekiel reacts to a proverb which ascribes present punishment to sins of the ancestors:

> Son of man, what is the meaning of this proverb that you recite in the land of Israel: 'Fathers have eaten green grapes, thus their children's teeth are on edge'? As I live, says the Lord God: I swear that there shall no longer be any-

> one among you who will repeat this proverb in Israel. For all lives are mine;
> the life of the father is like the life of the son, both are mine; only the one who
> sins shall die (Ezek 18:1-4).

God's universal power and his opposition to evil are primary in these and
other passages.[8]

Gnosticism was another attempt to account for the evil condition of
human existence in the world. It proposed not only an explanation of the
evil condition but also a mode of liberation from the evil situation. Gnosticism developed in the world of late antiquity and flourished in the early
centuries of the Church. Some forms of gnosticism were not influenced
by Judaism and Christianity; other forms drew upon Judeo-Christian
thought to fill out their systems; still other forms were actually Christian
systems with gnostic tendencies. Gnostic systems varied considerably in
their description of the heavenly realm and of the plight of humans. For
our purposes it will be helpful to cite their general tendencies and to select
one system, the *Apocryphon of John*, by way of example.

Gnosticism is an attempt to explain the human predicament of suffering and failure. It is a salvational movement that is designed to lift the
crushed spirits of humans beyond the darkness of this world to the su-
pernal kingdom of light. It is a movement of encouragement, powered
by the secret knowledge of the true derivation and destiny of humans.
Through a process of knowledge (*gnosis*) humans return to a realm from
which they have fallen. Humans find themselves in an evil situation, not
through personal fault, but through pre-cosmic events. "Original sin" is
not the fault of humans but the fault of powers that pre-exist the formation of humankind. Humans actually belong to a realm of light which is
above and beyond the worldly realm of darkness. They stem from light
but find themselves presently immersed in the flesh of the body and in
the darkness of this world.

The gnostic systems typically establish a rift between the realm of
the ineffable God and the sphere of lower powers and humans. The God
of the gnostics is extremely remote and does not come into contact with
the world. The transmundane God is the source of the lower god or gods
but these exist at a distance from the invisible God and do not know his
name. Gnostic literature depicts, sometimes in extremely colorful and
minute detail, the numerous archons and powers that exist as creations
of the lower gods. The powers do not coexist in a peaceable manner; they
engage in battle with each other and also with the powers of light. In some
gnostic systems the powers of darkness overcome the powers of light and
succeed in capturing for themselves a share of the light. The lower powers
(sometimes only the demiurge), not the transcendent God, create and
rule the world. They form humans to detain the light, to immerse it in a
realm of darkness and corruption. The human spirit (*pneuma*) stems

from the realm of light, but the powers thrust it into a fleshly and psychic body to ensure its imprisonment. The human body and the psychic passions are regarded as evil, for they detain the spark of light in a state of sleep and ignorance, and they prevent it from rising to its natural home in the realm above.

> There is a voluntary element in the downward movement of the divine: a guilty 'inclination' of the Soul (as mythical entity) toward the lower realms, with various motivations such as curiosity, vanity, sensual desire, is the gnostic equivalent of original sin. The fall is a pre-cosmic one, and one of its consequences is the world itself, another the condition and fate of the individual souls in the world.[9]

The sexual dimension of humans is especially evil, for it results in the propagation of humankind and the multiplication of lightsome sparks in a vast number of bodies. The female form is particularly dangerous because it lures men into sexual intercourse and provides the basis of human reproduction and dispersion of light. The light itself remains undiminished, just as a pearl cast in mud remains intact and pure.

Humans find themselves in this dire situation through the machinations of the gods, not through a fault of their own. They are subject to fatalistic powers beyond their control. Their only hope for escape from this evil world is *gnosis*, remembrance of their heavenly origin and knowledge of the way provided by the enlightenment of a savior, often identified as Christ. They seek release from the domination of evil and freedom to pass through heavenly spheres to a transcendent unity in the realm above. While the body and soul, inclined as they are toward evil, perish in death, the human spirit, that spark of light, seeks its natural home in the kingdom of light.[10]

The *Apocryphon of John* is relatively complete as an example of a gnostic system.[11] The author of the work, writing possibly in the second century of the Christian era, states that the risen Christ reveals to John, the son of Zebedee, the whole range of beings and the whole cycle of human imprisonment and liberation. The invisible Monad, the Spirit-Father and pure light, remains unnameable, but Pronoia (or Ennoia), the personification of his thought and the image of the invisible, comes forth from this Father of everything. The Pronoia is also called Barbelo. Many aeons, including the only-begotten one (Christ) and the mind (Sophia), are created. Now Sophia wishes to bring forth a likeness without the consent of the invisible one and without her consort. She indeed brings forth a form, but not her likeness. It is the monster Yaltabaoth, a lion-faced serpent, who receives great power from his mother. He is the chief archon, and he in turn creates other aeons, authorities, and angels. Yaltabaoth has a share of his mother's light, but he does not impart this light to his creations. Yaltabaoth boasts of his power and even assumes that only his mother is above him. Sophia notices her diminishment of life and she repents of her action. God makes his voice heard: this causes Yalta-baoth and his authorities to tremble. They see the form of God's image in the water. They scheme, then, to have the image become light for them: "Come, let us create a man according to the image of God and according to our likeness, that his image may become a light for us."[12] They create man (Adam) in the image of God (mirrored on the water) and in their own image. They create the soul and the body of man but he is still motionless. When Sophia wishes to retrieve the power which she gave to Yaltabaoth, she petitions God for help. He sends five lights down to induce Yaltabaoth to blow into the face of man some of his own spirit. Man receives the mother's power that goes out from Yaltabaoth. Man becomes greater than all, both Yaltabaoth and the others who create him. There ensues a struggle between the powers of light and the powers of darkness. In jealousy the archons throw Adam into the lowest region of matter. But God sends Epinoia to abide with Adam in a hidden fashion; Epinoia teaches Adam about the descent of his seed and about the way of ascent. The jealous archons fetter him in matter and place him in paradise to eat deceptive and deadly fruit of the tree of life. Yaltabaoth brings woman out of Adam, and she is made in the likeness of the Epinoia who is present with her. Through the Epinoia Christ teaches Adam and Eve to eat of the tree of knowledge. In a spirit of envy Yaltabaoth expels them from paradise. He instills sexual desire in Eve. Adam begets children and humans are multiplied; as a result, light is dispersed and made more difficult to recapture. Christ reminds humans of their divine origin. Only those who have this knowledge and the Spirit of life can ascend to the realm of light.

Another dualistic system was Manichaeism, doctrines developed by and under the name of Mani (AD 216?-276/277). Manichaeism was syncretistic, drawing together teachings of Buddha, Jesus, Zarathustra, and the prophets. As a dualistic system Manichaeism proposed to solve the problem of evil by postulating two uncreated principles: an evil principle of darkness and a good principle of light (the Father of light, or light as divine). The evil principle was not just the absence of light but was constituted by a positive or real quality of evilness.

The myths of the Manichaean religion point to a time in the beginning (before the existence of heaven and earth) when the two principles are separate and equal. The forces of darkness catch a glimpse of the light and are filled with envy. They rally their strength and attack the realm of light. The principle of light, thus roused to action, meets the challenge by producing the primal man and his sons to do battle with the forces of darkness. The sons of light are conquered and consumed by the sons of darkness. The Father of greatness through the living spirit eventually rescues primal man; but as this man is freed, some of his soul (his light portions) is left behind in the cosmos (in the soil, trees, animals, plants, water and fire). When the living spirit makes the cosmos from the parts of defeated powers of darkness, some light portions are rescued and are designed as sun, moon, and stars. The Father of greatness also creates a messenger to set the spheres in revolving motion; the revolution liberates light trapped in the cosmos. The powers of darkness meet the challenge from the realm of light by the creation of Adam and Eve. Adam's lust for Eve results in children and in the dispersal of light in human beings. Humans, in fact, whose design and sex are devilish, constitute the very battleground of light and darkness. Their bodies are foul prisons for their souls, exiled from the paradise of light. The soul is really a share of the divine life, a part of the divine light. While it exists in its present condition, the living soul or the living self is subject to sufferings in this world.

The Manichaean myth is very explicit:

> And (part) of that Light and Goodness of God that through (lit. from) fruits and buds was mixed with that progeny of Mazans, was bound into this body as a soul. And in it (i.e., the body of the first man) was inserted their greed and lust, salaciousness and copulation and enmity and calumny, envy and sinfulness, wrath and impurity, . . . and wickedness of soul and doubt, stealing and lying, robbery and ill-doing, obstinacy (?) and . . . , revenge and . . . sorrow and grief, pain and tooth-ache, poverty and begging, illness and old age, stench and brigandage (?).[13]

Jesus, who is sent from the realm of light, instructs Adam (that is, provides him with *gnosis*) about his origin and destiny; at the same time, all the captive light of the cosmos is regarded as the suffering Jesus. The history of humankind is thus the history of the suffering Jesus who collects himself out of the world. Salvation consists in the gathering of the divine particles of light from humans and from the whole cosmos. Salvation by way of knowledge (*gnosis*) occurs through a process of liberation of light from matter and the return of particles of light to the paradise of light.

The Manichaean community includes the elect and the hearers. The elect assist the hearers to achieve salvation. The hearers bring gifts to the elect, especially food for the daily meal. The meal is a way of releasing light from the fruits of the earth, therefore, it is taken with great caution. The hearers may receive liberation after death, either immediately after death or through a transmigration of souls. But it is especially Jesus who is the good doctor, the instructor in knowledge for the liberation of light (the self) from the world. In the final stage (the eschatological age) the principle of light will once again be separate from the principle of darkness, and the cosmos will be destroyed, though it seems that a portion of light (of God himself!) will never be freed from the power of darkness.[14]

The Manichaean system places the origin of evil and sin outside of human deliberation. in an uncreated principle of darkness. It exculpates humans, for they are not responsible for the evilness of their material body. They are morally responsible, however, when they choose not to free themselves from matter, when they refuse to proceed to the realm of light.

The Fathers of the Church responded to Manichaeism with the doctrine that there is only one Creator of the whole universe. Nothing is beyond the power of the one Lord. The problem of evil remained for them, but it was not solved by postulating an evil principle equal and opposite to the good principle. Nor was it solved by branding as evil the corporal, in particular, the sexual aspect of humans.

The Fathers also opposed the thinking that placed the sufferings and evil of the world in a kind of cyclical and astral fatalism. In this view the rhythm of nature or the stars causes catastrophes and evils; humans cannot avoid the evil happenings that are parceled out to them by the repetitive occurrences of nature or the will of the stars.[15]

Classical Greek literature often viewed humans as the victims of God's caprice. For no apparent reason, other than the willfulness of the gods, humans suffer a fate of dispossession and destruction. Humans could respond only by mute acceptance of the fate or by trying to neutralize the divine power. Christian authors reacted to this Greek theme by defending the native good intentions and activities of God.

Through the centuries theologians and Church authorities continued to confront threats to the uniqueness of the Creator and the goodness of creation. An important decree was issued at the most splendid of medieval councils. The IV Council of Lateran (1215), reacting to Albigensian and Catharist movements, declared the goodness of all creation and the unicity of the Creator:

> We firmly believe and directly confess that there is only one true God. . . . the one principle of the universe; the Creator of all things visible and invisible, spiritual and corporeal, who from the beginning of time by his omnipotent power created at the same time and out of nothing both the spiritual and the corporeal creature, that is to say, the angelic and the earthly and thereafter the human, who, as it were, shares in both, being composed of spirit and body.[16]

A long tradition of the Church identifies demonic power as an inducement to sin, if not the very power of sin. The Genesis account of creation (the earlier Yahwist account) includes a dialogue between Adam and Eve and a "talking serpent." Though a creature of the one God, the serpent proposes tantalizing options to the first couple. He does not force their decision, though he holds out an attractive but disobedient mode of action. The Yahwist writer relates that Adam and Eve choose the forbidden alternative and are punished for their choice; and the serpent too is punished for his part in the drama. While a literal interpretation of the account does not do justice to the dramatic character of the story, it is difficult to determine whether the author's strict message includes a definite reference to an outside influence on human failure.

Christian doctrine carefully maintains the universality of God's creative power. It holds that God is the unique source of all creatures, including the demonic powers. The demonic powers are limited—so it is taught—for, while they can tempt people, they cannot coerce the human will.

The demonic powers, therefore, are not the cause of an evil will or an evil action. Traditionally, they are seen as hostile persuaders of sin but not the power of sinning itself. This doctrine still obtains, though recently there has been some question about the characterization of demonic powers as separate, volitional creatures. Many scriptural accounts are set in mythological language. The experience, as reinterpreted by the Bible, "is that things which are in origin created can develop into powers hostile to man. They determine human freedom in advance of every decision and therefore human beings can never be completely aware of them, let alone overcome them. They are responsible for the conflicts which characterize reality and for the tragic character of many situations."[17]

The Church has usually assumed the existence of angelic and demonic powers. IV Lateran Council, for example, says: "The devil and the other demons were indeed naturally good by God's creation, but they became evil of their own accord. Man, however, sinned at the prompting of the devil."[18] Still the church has not felt obliged to defend their existence in an explicit, definitive manner. "For this reason, theologians should ask themselves whether they can claim without qualification that this existence is 'de fide'."[19]

Christian teaching, therefore, while it came into existence and developed in the context of gnostic and Manichaean thought, proclaimed the integrity of the Creator God and the essential goodness of the cosmos. The teaching proclaimed that human existence in this world is not evil, but it acknowledged that individuals are surrounded by forces of temptation and that they sin of their own volition. But why do they sin? Whence evil? Is there a basic fault in humans? The search for an answer continued.

3. Human Failure and Essential Fault

a. *Augustine*

In matters of free will, evil, and sin, Saint Augustine (354-430) finds himself doing battle on two fronts. Against the Manichaeans, whose teachings he embraced in his early adult life, he defends the basic goodness of material creation, in particular the goodness of free will. Against the Pelagians he defends the idea of a fallen will, a will damaged in the sin of Adam. The Pelagians, too, combat Manichaean fatalism, and they insist strongly on the freedom and responsibility of the will to act morally, to lead a Christian life, to pursue the promises of perfection, to keep the commandments of God, and to break with a sinful past. They hold that it is possible for humans to remain sinless, to refrain from doing evil. Pelagius himself says: "For if . . . some people are reported to have lived just and holy lives even before the Law and long before the coming of the Lord, our Savior, how much more must it be believed that we are able so to live after his coming and illustrious example, since we have been equipped by the grace of Christ and have been reborn into a better person."[20] Caelestius, too, the Pelagian controversialist and systematizer, was accused of the teaching "that even before the coming of Christ there were men without sin."[21] Pelagius reasons that the opposite opinion (it is not possible to be without sin) makes it appear that sin is a dimension of our human nature just as eating and drinking are natural functions.[22]

Augustine does not attempt to seek the origin of freedom itself, for he regards this as a vain pursuit. But, aware of the terrifying character of evil, he seeks to discover why humans act evilly. Why do humans oppose the will and law of God? Why are they egoistic, self-centered, and proud? Why do they worship self as an idol? It is not that free will is itself evil; such a Manichaean position disparages God's creation, indeed, the goodness of God himself. Yet the will is a creature, made from nothingness. It is capable of tending toward nothingness. It is capable of deflecting from its proper good and goal. Augustine examines this question in a discussion of lapsed angels; his reasoning, however, applies equally well to sinful humans. He holds that it is a fault (*vitium*) not to adhere to God.[23] Just as sight naturally belongs to the eyes or hearing to the ears, so also adherence to God pertains to angelic nature.[24] Why does the will turn away from God? How can the good that God creates be a cause of evil? Augustine simply says that the turning away from God is itself wicked: "When the will abandons the higher reality and turns to the lower, it becomes evil, not because the thing to which it turns is evil but because the turning itself is perverse. Therefore, the lower reality does not make the will evil, but the will has become evil in seeking the lower reality wickedly and inordinately."[25] What is the effective cause of the evil will? Augustine holds that there is none: "Let no one, therefore, seek an effective cause of the evil will; for it [the cause] is not effective, but defective, because the will itself is not effecting anything, but it is a deficiency. For defection from that which supremely is to something of less reality—this is to begin to have an evil will."[26] The good itself cannot be a cause of evil, yet there must be good in order to have a defect of good.

The will is capable of turning to its own works in pride and self-centeredness, and that is sin. It is capable of turning toward self and thus toward the nothingness from which it is made. It is capable of destructive self-love that rises up against God, the supreme good.[27] In his *Confessions* Augustine calls wickedness a perversion of the will, not a substance in itself as the Manichaeans contend: "And I sought the essence of wickedness, but I discovered no substance. Instead I found a perversion of the will: it turns aside from you, O God, the supreme substance, and toward the lowest realities; and becoming puffed up it abandons its inmost realities."[28] Fault or vice (*vitium*) characterizes the will when it pursues its own ends to the neglect of the proper order and the divine commands. Disorder and malfunction are at hand. Evil is formed by the corruption of the good. It is a privation of a good order that should be present. It is a defect, a lack, a deficiency, a privation of good (*privatio boni*). The human will can be defective precisely because it is contingent; it is made from nothingness.

Augustine says that Adam and Eve were already evil when they transgressed the commandment of God: "They began to be wicked in secret; as a result they fell into open disobedience. The evil act would not have come about if the evil will had not preceded it. Now what other than pride can be the beginning of an evil will?"[29] Augustine is not saying that Adam was created with a corrupt nature. He holds that pride preceded the actual disobedience. A proud pursuing of self rather than God results in a "corrupt tree." The will turned to evil is the source of open disobedience. Augustine does not explain the mystery of an evil will; he is content to note that the vice of the will is made possible by its creation from nothingness: "Now, nature could not have been corrupted by vice if it had not been made out of nothing."[30]

Augustine pictures the life of Adam and Eve in paradise as a privileged state of friendship with God, of immortality, of knowledge, of integrity (the subjection of the flesh to the will and of the will to God). But through sin the first parents lost the paradisiacal state for themselves and for their posterity. The whole of humankind is affected by the first sin because all humans stem from Adam and exist in him: "For all of us were in that one man when all of us were that one man who fell into sin by the woman who was made from him before the sin."[31] Their nature was altered for the worse and vitiated, and they subsequently handed on this nature to their posterity. They incurred a culpability that was passed on to all humans, "a sin which in one man became common to all."[32] It is an inherited culpability that deserves punishment: "As the apostle says, 'in Adam all die' (1 Cor 15:22); from him the beginning of the offense of God leads to the whole human race. All humankind is a certain mass of sin, owing a debt of punishment to the divine and highest justice. There is no iniquity [in God] whether it [the debt] is demanded or remitted."[33] Original sin, therefore, is voluntary in the will of Adam. "Through the evil will of that one man all sinned in him since all were that one man; therefore, from him each person derives original sin."[34] Original sin is a sin in Adam, but it is also the sin of his posterity by reason of his will.

Augustine recites the disastrous consequences of Adam's sin for the whole of humankind. He views the whole human race as damnable in the sight of God, as remote from his friendship, and as subject to sufferings and death. A person cannot enter the world without the taint of sin, without the "contagion of carnal generation."[35] Humans born into the world inherit both the guilt (*reatus*)[36] and the punishment of Adam's sin, even if they are born of baptized parents. The human situation of sin is summed up in the word "concupiscence" (*concupiscentia*), a disorderly desire. While Augustine is able to interpret concupiscence in the more natural sense of a physical feeling and desire, he regards it primarily and specifically as a vice and a sin. It is called a sin because it is caused by sin and it leads to sin. It is an insubordinate and guilty desire that opposes the will of God and the proper conduct of humans. Concupiscence characterizes the state of humankind suffering from the loss of God's good graces and existing in conflict with his law. The guilt (*reatus*) of concupiscence is removed in the sacrament of baptism, but the act (*actus*) remains in the regenerate as a torment and a temptation. The physical reality of concupiscence abides even in the baptized, but it is no longer imputed as sin. Augustine holds that it can be resisted only with the power of God:

> This concupiscence, which is expiated only by the sacrament of regeneration, assuredly transfers a bond of sin to the descendants, and this by a process of generation; but they are also loosed from it by a process of regeneration. For this concupiscence indeed is no longer sin in the regenerate, that is, when they do not yield to it and pursue illicit works and when their mind in its directive capacity does not offer its members to accomplish the works.... But since in a certain manner of speaking it [concupiscence] is called sin both because it came about as a result of sin and it produces sin if it gets the upper hand, its guilt prevails in the one who is born by way of nature. The grace of Christ, through the remission of all sins in the regenerate, does not allow this guilt to prevail if the person does not obey it [concupiscence] when in a certain fashion it demands evil works.[37]

Later in the same work Augustine's language is bolder and more liable to misinterpretation. Why does the concupiscence of the flesh remain in the baptized person? Augustine responds: "the concupiscence of the flesh is remitted in baptism, not that it does not exist but that it is not counted as sin."[38] One could get the impression that sin remains but is not imputed as sin; however, the more direct understanding, in view of the immediate context (the remission of the guilt), seems to be that the sin is remitted and that the remaining concupiscence is not reckoned as sin.

Original sin in Adam's posterity signifies that the human individual is not free to achieve righteousness. The person is not deprived of free will (*liberum arbitrium*), but he or she is really a slave to sin, has no freedom (*libertas*) in matters that pertain to personal salvation, and can only choose evil: "But who of us will say that by the sin of the first man free will (*liberum arbitrium*) perished from the human race? Freedom (*libertas*) indeed perished through sin, but it was that freedom which existed in paradise: the freedom of having full justice with immortality; for this reason human nature needs divine grace."[39] It is Christ who frees the will to choose the gospel and eternal life. Augustine puts the matter in words that border on determinism: "Without us he [God] brings it about that we will; but when we will and thus bring our will to act, he cooperates with us."[40] This bold language is typical of Augustine's choice for the overpowering sovereignty of God in the attempt to explain or to reconcile the relationship between grace and free will.

The state of perdition is so universal that infants cannot be born without "the contagion of sin."[41] Infants, too, need regeneration, and for this reason the Church baptizes them unto the remission of sins. Children who die without baptism do not gain the vision of God but suffer positive punishments, even if they are the mildest of punishments: "Who would doubt that non-baptized infants, since they have only original sin and not the burden of personal sins, will experience the lightest condemnation of all?"[42]

b. *Thomas Aquinas*

Saint Thomas Aquinas (1225-1274) builds upon Aristotelian thought and Augustinian tradition to elaborate a doctrine of evil as an aspect of the concept of privation, a concept that he finds in both Aristotle and Augustine. For Aristotle privation is one of the formal principles of generation; privation is the negative starting point for anything that comes to be; it is required for the appearance of any new form. The appearance of one form depends on the "corruption" of another.

Thomas, then, views evil (*malum*) as a privation, as the absence of good. Evil is not simple negation but rather the lack of some perfection or form that ought to be present, the lack of proper direction in an action, the lack of a measure that ought to be there. Evil is not a separate subject in itself; it can only exist in some being that is itself good. Now the evil of sin is the act that lacks the form, the direction, or the measure that it ought to have. An evil is present when an action falls short of its proper and required goal; this evil then becomes a fault (*culpa*) when the will is responsible for the failure. "In volitional matters the defect of an action proceeds from the will which acts deficiently inasmuch as in acting it does not submit itself to its measure. The defect, however, is not a fault; but the fault follows when the will acts with such a defect."[43]

The evil of sin involves the lack of goodness that should characterize human action. Thomas searches for some reason why there is this failure, this lack of perfection. The universe is a scale of beings—from the exaltedness of God to the lowliness of material reality and all kinds of intermediate beings. Thomas says, "Just as the perfection of the whole universe requires that there be not only some incorruptible beings but also some corruptible ones, so too the perfection of the universe requires that some things are able to fail in goodness; it follows that sometimes they do fail."[44] The failure of some things is not without value; for some good stems from failure. Thomas notes, for instance, that there would be no patience if there were no injustice in the world.[45] In these deliberations on evil Thomas does not imply that humans necessarily and willfully fail. As he searches and strains for an understanding of the evil in the world, he discovers some intelligibility of evil, some "reasons" why there is moral failure, even though the "reasons" do not guide him far into the mystery of evil.

A basic aspect of evil is original sin. Thomas uses the thought categories of privation and cause (formal, material, agent) to define the nature of original sin. The formal element of original sin is the privation of original justice: the loss of the gift of integrity (freedom from concupiscence) and the loss of divine friendship. The material element of original sin is concupiscence. "Thus, therefore, the privation of original justice, by which the will was subject to God, is the formal element in original sin. Every other disorder of the powers of the soul is a certain material element of original sin."[46] It is clear that original sin is not merely a lack of original justice; it is also a disordered disposition of nature. More precisely, because it is a lack of original justice, it involves a disharmony in human nature. Original sin is "a certain disordered disposition resulting from the dissolution of that harmony which was once the essence of original justice . . . ."[47] Since original sin is a corrupt disposition of nature itself, it can be called a sin of nature (*peccatum naturae*).[48] This does not mean that human nature itself is evil, but it means that the evil of sin makes its appearance right in human nature as a corrupt disposition, an inclination to an inordinate act, a disordered disposition which should not be present according to the original intention of God.

The agent cause of original sin is not God, who can only create the good, nor is it the devil, who can only suggest and tempt. The cause of sin is found within the human heart, within Adam first, then within his posterity. Sin occurs in the will of Adam, who chooses to oppose the divine command. It is relatively easy for Thomas to characterize original sin as voluntary in Adam, but more difficult to find reasons for the voluntariness of original sin in Adam's posterity. To illustrate the universal voluntariness of original sin in Adam's children, he resorts to the image of humankind as one huge individual, composed of body and soul. Just as the members of one body are moved by the will, so also all the members of humankind are moved by the will of Adam. "In this way, then, the disorder which is in this man born of Adam is voluntary, not by his own will, but by the will of his first parent, who, by a process of generation, moves all who originate from him, even as the soul's will moves to action all the [body's] members."[49] The analogy of the body helps Thomas to explain the willful character of original sin and also its culpable spread to all people. It helps him to illustrate his teaching that Adam's posterity is not only struck by the evil of punishment (*malum poenae*) but also by the evil of fault (*malum culpae*). The analogy also assists Thomas to explain the transmission of original sin; the instrumental cause of original sin is generation, or more specifically, the corporal seed of man.[50]

As a sin of nature, finally, Thomas notes the wounds that original sin inflicts on human nature. It causes ignorance in the mind, malice in the will, concupiscence in the concupiscible powers (those that are oriented toward the sensible good), and weakness in the irascible powers (those that are oriented toward the difficult). The first power to be touched by original sin is the will, but the powers most infected are the concupiscible powers.[51] In sum, original sin touches the whole of the human person, depriving him or her of the loving grace of God and producing an inclination toward evil. The consequences of original sin are thus viewed against the backdrop of the paradisiacal life of divine friendship and harmony.

Infants that die in a state of original sin do not suffer positive punishments but "only" a privation of the beatific vision. They exist without any exterior or interior pain, in a condition of natural happiness. They do not mourn their exclusion from eternal glory because they do not know it.[52]

c. Hegel

Philosophers, too, find it necessary to deal with the problem of evil in the world. Their reflections tend to be all-inclusive, ranging from comments on the evils of natural disasters to the failures of willful malice. We choose to sketch the philosophical reflections of Georg W. F. Hegel (1770-1831), and this for a number of reasons. Hegel's system of thought, while not acceptable today as an account of human existence, greatly influenced the course of philosophical thinking for the last century and a half; in particular Karl Marx's positions were shaped by Hegel, even as he opposed Hegel's system. Hegel the philosopher was also a Christian of the Lutheran tradition; his philosophical system not only referred to themes of Christian doctrine but also attempted to account for them in a rational way. Finally, his themes of alienation and reconciliation are still significant for the ways in which people today understand their human predicament and its resolution in community.

Hegel provides an ontological account of the presence of evil in the world. His account of evil is placed in the context of a whole system of philosophical thought, and it becomes intelligible only within the framework of this system. His account is ontological, for it attempts to analyze and to express the reality of evil in the widest range of reflective reasoning.

Evil is a dimension of the structure of this universe; therefore, it must be accounted for by a comprehensive view of the whole—a view of the Absolute and of the manifestations of the Absolute.

The Hegelian model for understanding the Absolute is not just Substance, as Spinoza said, but also Subject. God is really Subject. But the Absolute as Subject does not exist in splendid isolation. The Absolute as Subject is very much involved in the process of the universe. The Absolute as Subject is immediately related to the objective elements of the universe; it goes beyond itself, externalizes itself, and enters into determinate beings as their inner structure and necessity. In fact, the Absolute as Subject is the principle of reasoned development in the whole world. There is a self-realization of the Subject through a positing of the objective and the particular, the solidity of external reality. The Subject posits its opposite and thereby becomes a principle of movement, unrest, and reflection; for the positing of the opposite is the place where the Subject can negate the opposite and thereby effect a return in self-assertion.[53]

A principle of Reason is at work in the world. Reason governs the world and guides the larger plan of world history. History itself is the self-realization of Reason in the spatial and temporal dimensions of the world. History discovers a Reason that is at work in the various states of the development of the world.

The Absolute as Subject is not indeterminate as is that of the Romantics. The Romantics propose an immediate intuition of the Absolute, but the intuition provides only an indefinite vision of God. The Hegelian Absolute is a God who is not beyond the beings of this world but one who is involved and embodied in this world. The Absolute shows itself in this world; in fact, it must show itself by reason of its very structure. The Absolute as God necessarily creates the beings of this world. It is always positing its opposite and becomes conscious of self through the elements of the world, in particular, through human beings who are the vehicles of his existence and will. The world, therefore, is the self-manifestation of God. He is active in the world and the world itself is in God. The Absolute actualizes itself through all the stages of world history and only finds its consummation at the end of the development.[54] To know the whole of the being of the world is to know it as infinite; it is to know it as the being and activity of God. To know God is to know the whole of reality.

Hegel's most characteristic term is Mind or Spirit (*Geist*). The substance of the whole is really Spirit. It is cosmic Spirit that posits the world by a necessary process of creation. The Spirit necessarily moves in the world and becomes the power of the whole. The Spirit is necessarily embodied in the finite beings of the universe. It is expressed in the individuals of the universe and in their self-realizations; thus, it becomes the objective Spirit in the development of history and politics. It is the Spirit, for instance, of the rational state. The goal of the whole process of the Spirit's passage through the world is self-knowledge. The Spirit must become self-knowing. But it does not achieve this goal except through a process of development: it moves from a state of being in itself to otherness; the determinate otherness that it posits is really a self-estrangement, a being for self, an alienation; but the process continues until the Spirit reaches a stage of being in and for itself. In this third stage the Spirit has returned to itself, has become certain of itself, is conscious of itself.[55] What happens in this whole dialectical process is that the Spirit integrates the whole of the universe in itself; the Spirit is completely immanent in the parts of the universe and thus is able to draw them all to the point of completion. The basic opposition or alienation or split in the world is overcome by the integrating force of the Spirit. The Spirit is, therefore, the power of the reconciliation of the whole.

There is a certain rational necessity in the structure of the whole; the necessity is not merely in thought but also in determinate things. There is a certain Notion or Concept (*Begriff*) that governs the whole universe. The Concept is revealed in the particular structures of things and, in fact, is the ground of all multiplicity. The Concept is the grasp of the whole process, a grasp which is at the same time at the basis of all things and which governs the whole by a process of internal necessity. This Concept is manifest in thought and in the ontological reality of all things.

The inner reason of all reality may also be called the Idea. The Idea is expressed and externalizes itself in nature and in history through the operation of the Spirit. The particular things that are expressed by the Spirit in a movement of contradiction are themselves expressions of the Idea. The Idea may be regarded as the starting point of the whole necessary movement. In the end the Absolute Idea returns to a unity of self-knowing truth.

Hegel's system is designed to solve one of the perennial problems of philosophy: the reconciliation of freedom with the objectivity and rationality of the world. It is evident to him that human freedom abides in the face of objective nature. Hegel accounts for the relationship between freedom and nature by expressing their basic unity. Freedom is basically the freedom of the Spirit; and the human expression of the Spirit is conformity to the movement of the cosmic Spirit. The human will discovers its identity and duty by conforming to the Spirit that governs the movement of history, e.g., by following the expression of Spirit in the ways of political society. The movement of the Spirit, in fact, leads to absolute freedom, the complete return of Spirit to self in the goal of absolute freedom.

The necessary movement of Spirit in the particular beings of this world (creation) is itself evil because the particulars are remote from the universal goal. It is clear that Hegel views evil as ontologically necessary, as an inevitable dimension of the finite. The finite and the particular are evil because they are distant from the universal. As a dimension of the finite, evil exists wherever there is particular action, wherever there is the movement of Spirit in the world; while no action at all is innocence.[56] There is a necessary amount of evil in the particular, cut off as it is from the universal and from the return of the Spirit to itself. Insofar as the particular is cut off from the universal, it exists in a state of alienation which necessarily involves guilt. The human being is involved in evil (the fall) by self-centeredness, by becoming other than self in thought, by becoming other than the Good. Otherness is the birth of self-consciousness, and this otherness results in the evil of alienation.[57] The original sin, therefore, is the affirmation of the particular, the affirmation of the self as particular, the expression of self as different from the universal. Consequently, the fall is unavoidable since it results from the finite will that is ranged against the will of the Spirit. The fall of Adam in the Genesis story symbolizes this turn against the universal. Where there is self-centeredness in the existence of the particular form of the Spirit, where there are any particular intentions and goals, there is a condition of evil, a condition that is opposed to the direction of the whole. To retreat into self is evil because it is remote from the Spirit. Self-centeredness is evil.

Alienation is a central feature of Hegel's system. Alienation is the otherness of opposition, and oppositions are found in all areas of the universe. There is the separateness of everything from its opposite in nature, self, others, and the infinite. There is the otherness of the thing that is present for consciousness. There is the otherness of consciousness that is aware of the object. There is the alienation of defining self in the other self or society. There is the otherness of self-consciousness that seeks its opposite in recognition.[58] There is the otherness of the finite that is posited by the Spirit in its movement through the world. The development of the Spirit in the world necessarily involves the positing of the other and the foreign. The Spirit thus becomes estranged from itself and it expressed in the particular forms of the universe. The Spirit as self-consciousness becomes alienated in the world. It is self-estrangement since the Spirit itself posits its own otherness in the movement through otherness to self-certainty.

Another form of opposition or alienation is the master-slave relationship. Both master and slave seek recognition and integrity in the other. But while the master is independent and enjoys what the slave prepares for him or her, the slave is dependent and must prepare things for the enjoyment of the master while seeking recognition in the works of his or her labors. But there is a reversal here. In finding no resistent otherness in the slave, the master stagnates and becomes a plain self-consciousness without any thrust to the universal. Moreover, the master becomes a servant because he or she depends on the labors of the slave and thereby takes up a mediate relationship to the world. The slave, however, finds integrity and independent consciousness in the otherness of his or her work and in the otherness of the master; the slave thereby comes to recognition and mastery.[59]

Alienation is also verified in the unhappy consciousness which charactizes the person in this world. The unhappy consciousness recognizes itself as independent, free, and immutable, yet as subject to the contradiction of the other, to the mutability of the world.

Another kind of alienation is the identification of the person with external social reality. The person necessarily exists in a society but finds that he or she must identify with the external customs and features of a society.

There is also alienation in forms of religion. The Spirit is expressed in various forms of religion, but these forms are unstable. The forms themselves exist in otherness, in alienation from the Spirit, and they require a continual movement of contradiction and unity to move toward the goal of self-certainty of the Spirit.

What is significant in all of this is that contradiction or alienation is required for all life and movement. It is only by a continual process of opposition that the movement of the Spirit through history is possible. There is the positing of the opposite which in turn is overcome or transcended. Contradiction underlies the whole Hegelian movement from the positing of the other on the part of the Spirit to the movement towards its self-certainty. It is the task of religion, but especially of philosophy, to overcome the divisions and oppositions of reality in order to bring about reconciliation and union.

Hegel shares the Romanticists' desire for unity and wholeness. Hegel's whole system of thought is directed to a point of unity where the sundry oppositions of the universe will be overcome (the oppositions of Spirit, nature, self, and all particulars). He seeks a point of unity where the infinite and the finite will be overcome and reconciled. It is the Absolute that will ultimately bring about the reconciliation between identity and contradiction, between the unchangeable and the individual. The opposition is overcome first in thought, through dialectical thinking, but also in the Incarnation. Hegel uses the Christian theme of the Incarnation to show that the cosmic Spirit and the finite spirit are joined in one person. But the Incarnation itself is overcome as Jesus dies, is raised up, and returns to the Father. Thereafter the Incarnation continues as the Spirit is sent upon the church and provides a source of life. At the present time the various religious cults and practices function as a means of bringing about unity even as they express a diversity. But the truest agent of reconciliation is philosophy, for philosophy ultimately effects reconciliation of the observer and the observed, of the observer and reality. Philosophy ultimately accounts for the goal of the whole movement of Spirit in history: it is the self-knowing *Geist*. Thus there are various agents of reconciliation and forgiveness: the Spirit that is moving through the course of history to the goal of self-knowledge; the dialectical mode of thinking characteristic of his philosophy, the Incarnation and religious cults, moral efforts at union, the various movements of forgiveness, and finally the passage of the Absolute that brings about the identity of subject and object.

Religion is not just a feeling of dependence, as Schleiermacher maintains, but it is an objective and representational expression of the Spirit. Religion expresses the Spirit's drive toward rational self-revelation. The movement of the Spirit is expressed in cultural images and pictorial representations (*Vorstellungen*). Consequently religion is subject to an evolution of images, symbols, and representations, coming finally to Christianity, the absolute form of religion. But ultimately religion must be transcended, for it must culminate in philosophy. Religion, even in its Christian form, is a less adequate expression of the absolute Spirit than philosophy. Ultimately, religion will be overcome when the Spirit reaches the goal of final self-consciousness and absolute knowing.[60]

It is clear to Hegel that the Christian revelation must be known by the religious consciousness of humans; faith without rational insight must give way to an understanding by reason. Faith, in fact, represents one aspect of the alienated self. It is also the externalization of the Spirit in the believer. Through religious representations and images one understands the movement of the Spirit in the world.

The community of individuals is also an expression of the Spirit. In community individuals realize their highest form of moral existence. In community the scattered individuals are brought into a form of unity. Community is the mediation between abstract humankind and the multiplicity of individuals in the world. The community bears the customs of a society and offers the highest form of consciousness. The state is the highest realization of human community. It is the state that expresses the absolute Idea. It is the state that realizes the common good and hands on the customary benefits of society.

The community that is Christianity is the point of unity between God and humankind, between the infinite and the finite. Here the revelation of God in his Spirit is grasped and understood. Here Jesus receives a resurrection from the dead.

The culmination of history is the community embodiment of Spirit. The Spirit endeavors to bring the whole movement of history to its final goal in a community of Spirit and individuals.

d. *Teilhard de Chardin*

Pierre Teilhard de Chardin (1881-1955), the French Jesuit and pale-ontologist, is committed to the basic goodness of the evolving cosmos. Surprisingly—given his traumatic experience of World War I—he pays relatively little attention to sin and evil in his system of thought. His guiding preoccupation is the unity of Spirit and matter and the reconciliation of Christian doctrine with the norms of evolutionary biology. As a dedicated Christian and a devoted scientist, he endeavors to discover the ultimate unity of the two commitments. From Christian doctrine, especially from the writings of Saint Paul, he accepts the idea that the glorified Christ, the transfigured Christ who hands over the kingdom to the Father (1 Cor 15:28), is the ultimate goal of human striving and expectation. From evolutionary biology he accepts the idea that the universe is in continual development. He holds, moreover, that the evolutionary process is directed orthogenetically toward an end: the Omega Point.

The tendency towards unified complexity, consciousness, and love in the form of attractive energy begins with the smallest particles of reality. The inner tendency within reality drives these particles to form ever greater and more elaborate configurations, ever more complex organisms, ever increased levels of consciousness. Through an evolutionary process of thousands of millions of years the universe has produced a self-reflective being in the figure of the human person. This is not to say that God's presence was absent from the process that resulted in the formation of the human species. His sustaining power is ever present; in fact, the power of Christ reaches back to provide the push or pull that sets the whole process—even from the beginning—on a goal-directed course: the Omega Point. The end, the Omega Point, is really the full Christ, the human-divine Christ and all who belong to him, the union of God and the world of creatures. In this way Teilhard finds that both Christian teaching and evolutionary science converge in one unified point: communion with God in Christ and in the world.

The whole universe in its cosmogenesis, biogenesis, and Christo-genesis is directed to the point of unity. The present condition of the universe, however, is one of disunity—rather, one of multiplicity. As early as 1917 he wrote that the multiple *"is at the root of all our evils."*[61] The multiple is a principle of evil. If unity is envisioned as the supreme goal, disunity or the multiple lies at the other extreme of the vision. To be is to be united; to be on a lower level of existence is to be divided. The more the division, the disunity, the multiple, the less the level of existence. The multiple is non-being, not in the metaphysical sense of nothing at all, but in the sense of unorganized multiplicity, of potentiality of union, of the opposite of being.[62] The multiple produces levels of non-being, pain, and sin, the traditional dimensions of evil. "Non-being, pain, sin—ontological evil, sensibly experienced evil, moral evil—these are *three aspects of the same evil principle*, whose reduction calls for an infinity of time, a principle that is ever being reborn—the Multitude."[63] Humans embody evil when they strive to stand apart in isolation and refuse selfishly to build up the community of peoples.

Teilhard describes the multiple as original sin, though he is not particularly happy with this suggestion. Another proposal is that the beginning manifests a non-sinful multiple but the drive toward unity entails the statistical necessity of suffering and error.[64] Multiplicity provides the very opportunity for chance and thus for evil. It is inevitable that evil, even moral evil, occurs in the passage from the multiple to the one. It can be said that the multiple itself is evil, for "the many" provide the possibility of evil. Evil becomes a statistical necessity in the evolutionary movement of the world. Evil is not simply an incidental feature of the whole process; it is necessarily involved in the progressive creation of the world. Evil becomes a by-product of the process of complexification and of unification.

Evil is really a waste of spiritual energy; it diverts the thrust of love from the unification of the Infinite to the disorder of the inadequate.

> If man fails to recognize the true nature and the true object of his love, the disorder which follows is profound and irremediable. Stubbornly trying to gratify a passion which opens on the Infinite with something that is simply inadequate, man desperately tries to make up for the fundamental disequilibrium brought about within him by a restless search for pleasures, especially those of a material character. This is vanity and, in the eyes of anyone who even partly perceives the inestimable value of the 'spiritual quantum' of mankind, a frightening waste.[65]

e. Tillich

The systematic theology of Paul Tillich (1886-1965) is in contact with the philosophical traditions of Plato and Aristotle, Aquinas and Hegel, Kierkegaard and Sartre. It is from these traditions as well as from his understanding of Saint Paul, Saint Augustine, and Martin Luther that he develops his theological view of the fall and sin of humans. The myth of the fall is crucial for him, since it determines the understanding of the conditions of human existence in the world.

Tillich wishes to follow the philosophical tradition which distinguishes between essence and existence in finite realities, especially in human beings. He notes that Plato separates the essential realm of eternal ideas from the existential realm of this world where there is mere opinion, error, and evil. He notes further that the Scholastics teach a split of essence and existence in humans, but not in God. He examines Hegel's essentialist position, namely, that existence is the actualization of essence, that the world is the self-realization of Spirit, but that ultimately there is no gap between essence and existence. Tillich rejects Hegel's essentialist position and follows rather the tradition of a Kierkegaard, a Marcel, and in general the existentialist movement of modern times.[66]

Tillich maintains the distinction between essence and existence in the realm of creation but not in God, for God is beyond this kind of separation. Humans live in a world where there is a clear rift between essence and existence. The essence is the ideal world; it indicates what the world should be; it is the truth about the world and humans. But the world of existence falls short of the ideal world. The symbol of the fall of Adam, in fact, expresses the situation as it is presently experienced by humans. Tillich demythologizes the symbol of the fall in terms of essence and existence, but it is a half-way demythologization because there is still a temporal element in the phrase (transition from essence to existence) and because complete demythologization is not possible when speaking of God.[67]

The human situation is one of estrangement from the essential realm. It is a participation in the essential realm, to be sure, but a participation mixed with distortion. Existence distorts the essential. Existential estrangement represents a fall from the essential goodness. "Whenever the ideal is held against the real, truth against error, good against evil, a distortion of essential being is presupposed and is judged by essential being."[68] From the very beginning creation is characterized by essence and existence, by an existential actualization of the essential goodness.

> Actualized creation and estranged existence are identical. . . . If God creates here and now, everything he has created participates in the transition from essence to existence. He creates the newborn child; but, if created, it falls into the state of existential estrangement. This is the point of coincidence of creation and the Fall. But it is not a logical coincidence; for the child, upon growing into maturity, affirms the state of estrangement in acts of freedom which imply responsibility and guilt. Creation is good in its essential character. If actualized, it falls into universal estrangement through freedom and destiny.[69]

Humans are endowed with freedom; that is, they can deliberate and decide, and they are responsible for their actions. But their freedom is exercised within definite limits, which Tillich calls destiny. Destiny establishes the conditions and parameters of freedom, the givens of personal endowments, nature, and history. One can attempt to place oneself above the finite limits of personal existence, but this is what Tillich calls *hubris*: a self-exaltation, a desire to be like God, a turning toward the self as the center of existence. In this endeavor the estrangement only increases.

The symbol of the fall points to the tragic and universal character of the world, which is marked by a transition from essence to existence. The individual act of freedom takes place within this world, within this destiny. Thus Tillich says, "In every individual act the estranged or fallen character of being actualizes itself."[70] Again, "Man is responsible for the transition from essence to existence because he has finite freedom and because all dimensions of reality are united in him."[71] The fall expresses the tragic character of human existence, in which there is an actual and existential distortion of essential goodness through the factors of human freedom, self-actualization, and destiny.

The fall is a cosmic event since it affects not only humans but also the whole universe. The split between essence and existence characterizes all creatures. The sin of humans finds its repercussions in the whole of reality.

> Just as, within man, nature participates in the good and evil he does, so nature, outside man, shows analogies to man's good and evil doing. Man reaches into nature, as nature reaches into man. They participate in each other and cannot be separated from each other. This makes it possible and necessary to use the term 'fallen world' and to apply the concept of existence (in contrast to essence) to the universe as well as to man.[72]

The fall places humans in estrangement from God, from the universe, and from themselves. Individuals exist in a condition of aloneness and separation. They find themselves at a distance from a nature which they cannot fully understand and from which they always remain remote. They find themselves at a distance from the very ground of their being.

Anxiety characterizes this human life. Anxiety is not the fear of particular objects of hate or violence; rather, it is the all-pervading awareness of finitude. It is an awareness of nonbeing, or an awareness of the threat of falling once again into nonbeing. Despair is the feeling of abandonment to this situation of conflict, the feeling that there is no way out of the situation. "The pain of despair is the agony of being responsible for the loss of the meaning of one's existence and of being unable to recover it."[73]

If "Adam" symbolizes the essential nature of humans, "Christ" symbolizes and provides the new reality, the new Being; he is the power that overcomes existential estrangement through the cross and resurrection. The atonement effected by Christ is the redemptive healing of the split between God and humans, between one person and another, between humans and the world. It is the task of courage to accept the participatory and contingent character of human existence even as one waits for the final manifestation of the new being in Christ.

f. Ricoeur

The philosopher Paul Ricoeur (b. 1913), working generally within the framework of phenomenology and hermeneutics, seeks the origin of evil and corruption in a pre-condition of human existence. He examines the various levels of disproportion that exist in the human person, in particular the duality of the voluntary and the involuntary, the duality of freedom and nature. His concern is not ontology but the phenomenological description of the free and the unfree of human existence. His study focuses precisely on the relationship between the voluntary and the involuntary, on the split between these two realities of human life. Thus, the willful choosing of evil as such is not the pre-condition of evil, though the decision for evil is itself morally evil.

Ricoeur discovers a fault, a rift at the very center of the human person. The fault is comparable to discontinuities between layers of the earth's structure; in fact, the geological rift is the image that lies behind Ricoeur's use of the word "fault." The fault in the human person is perceived as a dividedness, a flaw, an error. The fault as error is really fallibility that stems from the human composition. Humans are fragile, frail, fallible, and subject to error. "But to be fragile is not yet to break; the impetus plunging us into moral evil is not generated by our structures per se. And thus it cannot be blamed upon them. Finitude is not to be confused with guilt."[74] The fault is a division, a disproportion existing in the human person, but it is not yet moral corruption and guilt. It is, however, the locus of evil.

The fault or rift is seen especially in the division between the voluntary and the involuntary. But the split is expressed in other ways as well. It is evident in the polarity of the finite and the infinite. Within the human person there is a tension and disproportion between the finite and the infinite. There is a finitude of perspective[75] but an infinitude of volition. The will is free to affirm beyond the perspective of understanding. There is, for instance, a disproportion between happiness as an infinite end and pleasure as a particular and partial goal. Happiness is the end that fulfills all human activity; it is the end of all motivation. Pleasure is the fulfillment of particular desires. There are thus two kinds of terminations of affective movements: "pleasure, which fulfills or culminates or perfects particular acts or processes; and happiness, . . . perfection of the total work of man . . . ."[76] Ricoeur expresses the duality in these terms: "Thus it is the source of the extreme human disproportion: in human action, the tension between the finitude of character and the infinitude of happiness; character as origin and happiness as infinite end."[77]

Humans are not infinite, are not gods, and yet they conceive of desires that surpass their limit:

> . . . the era opened up to freedom by fault is a certain experience of infinity that hides from us the finite situation of the creature, the ethical finiteness of man. Henceforth the evil infinite of human desire—always something else, always something more—which animates the movement of civilizations, the appetite for pleasure, for possessions, for power, for knowledge—*seems* to constitute the reality of man.[78]

The fault is expressed in the self that proclaims itself morally and ontologically autonomous.[79] So also does imagination, the kind that can make an object fascinating and charming, express the condition of fault or provide the point of entry for fault: "But prior to being an invitation to the fault, imagination of pleasure is an attribute of actual pleasure which is secondary with respect to need."[80]

The fault also becomes evident in an alienation of self-consciousness in passion or in a "they." "Thus self-consciousness is relatively alienated, as in passion or in the 'they,' it constitutes a dialectic of rejection. On the other hand, it constitutes a dialectic of confirmation when consciousness is relatively its own mistress, as in the act of 'taking a stand.'"[81] Or again, "It is the fate of self-consciousness to corrupt itself in all the cases in which it becomes pure observer."[82] The individual fixes on the other, is externalized, and does not return to the self (cf. the Hegelian notion of alienation); or rather, the individual returns to the self only through the other.

The fault is manifest in the denial of freedom to myself: "I can hide my freedom from myself and lie to myself; by this denial which is one aspect of the fault, consciousness imitates the thing and hides behind it."[83] But the ultimate expression of fault is defiance. "At the core of refusal is defiance and defiance is the fault. To refuse necessity from below is to defy Transcendence."[84]

For Ricoeur, therefore, the origin of sin and moral evil is really a precondition that exists in the very center of humans. It is their capacity to fail. It is the split that constitutes fallibility. "To say that man is fallible is to say that the limitation peculiar to a being who does not coincide with himself is the primordial weakness from which evil arises."[85]

4. Evolution

The evolutionary origin of humankind has gained common acceptance during the past century or more. It is generally assumed that the human species developed from pre-existing living forms over a long period of time and that self-conscious humans appeared thousands, perhaps even millions of years ago. Paleontologists continue to revise backwards the time of the appearance of intelligent, human forms. Through a long period of advancement, through trial and error, the human species arrives at its present condition of life and intelligence.

It is possible to assume an evolutionary view of the human species as one attempts to account for the situation of sin in the world, especially the situation of original sin. An evolutionary interpretation of sin notes the primitive struggle of humans to develop their potential and to achieve the fulfillment of themselves through the cosmic forces available to them.

One version of the evolutionary interpretation of original sin holds that the condition of sin is actually the slow and imperfect development of humankind. As such, the evolutionary condition is built into the very makeup of the cosmos and is therefore beyond the pale of voluntary sin. It is the natural condition of humans to progress through evolutionary stages, to move from primitive forms to more complex forms of life. The struggle of the evolutionary process and the necessity of development in an evolutionary fashion are the very natural conditions of original sin: the sin of nature, not of will.[86]

This version of the evolutionary interpretation of sin may also include a reference to the instinctive drives of the human species, the drives which are designed to preserve and to protect life but which also result in injury or death to other living beings. The instincts of self-preservation and propagation bring the individual of the species into conflict with others for the selection of mates, for territory, for food and other goods of the earth. This conflict, which causes physical pain, mental suffering, and even death, is seen as the very means of evolutionary progress. The conflict is unfortunate but conforms to the very being of the cosmos. Instinctivists, for example, hold that a person's aggressive behavior "is due to a phylogenetically programmed, innate instinct which seeks for discharge and waits for the proper occasion to be expressed."[87] Even if one does not accept the notion of a destructive instinct or of a learned behavior of destruction, as Fromm does not, the evolutionary process still involves inevitable and destructive conflicts.

Another version of the evolutionary interpretation of original sin postulates the conscious and free decision not to cooperate with the process of development. Through ill will (sluggishness, envy, hate, etc.), a person refuses to further the cause of evolution. This condition of ill will characterized the very first humans who were capable of self-conscious and free decision. And it characterizes the human species since the beginning. Everyone more or less hinders the process of evolution, fails to assist the development of self, others, and the cosmos. It is this failure to realize one's own potential and the failure to assist in the realization of the potential of others that can be described as original sin.[88]

A more evident joining of scientific evolution and theological anthropology is represented by the position of Z. Alszeghy and M. Flick.[89] They postulate that original sin as a phenomenon reaching back to an event in the beginning of humankind resulted from a refusal to proceed to the next stage of evolution, namely, the stage of gracious dialogue with God. One couple that reached the threshold of this stage was destined to awaken humanity in other couples and did so from a deficient position, i.e., already deficient in the gracious relationship to God. One couple represented the many (corporate personality), even though the many did not stem from the one couple (biological polygenism).[90]

Juan Segundo, the Paraguayan theologian who pursues various themes of liberation theology, offers yet another version of the evolutionary interpretation of original sin. He sets up a comparison between the law of entropy (the conservation of energy) and various aspects of original sin (guilt, concupiscience, failure). While the total amount of energy of the universe is not lost, it can be degraded into simpler forms. "So if evolution tends toward ever more concentrated and powerful syntheses of energy, then it does so by running counter to the statistically greater tendency toward ever simpler syntheses of degraded energy."[91] Where there is little volitional directiveness on the part of humans in society, where there is degradation of energy among the masses, there is original sin.[92] Sin, in sum, is the aspect of egotism and disintegration that characterizes humans. "At the level where love clusters all the energies of the universe for their maximum potentialities we find entropy, almost imperceptible, taking the form of sin, that is, the easy road of egotism and routine that leads to disintegration."[94] Sin and enslavement to the world comprise the negative vector of evolution, while love and self-surrender comprise the positive vector.[95]

Since Teilhard's system cuts across many disciplines, it can be mentioned here as well. Perhaps his system belongs in the "evolutionary" category of explanation more than to any other. He is totally committed to the concept of biological evolution, and he devotes his energy to its integration into the Christian view of the cosmos. It is in the context of evolution that Teilhard speaks of evil and sin. Evil is an inevitable waste in the process of evolution; it is a statistical necessity. On the human level, use of freedom in the sphere of evolution inevitably leads to sin and failure (as it does also to good and success). The multiplicity of beings in the cosmos inevitably combine egocentricity and disunity: the very stuff of evil and sin.[96]

Before leaving this interpretation it might be helpful to cite a suggestion of Saint Irenaeus. He proposes that the human race was created in an immature and imperfect condition and that humans were obliged to grow and be brought to the state of perfection. But because of their immaturity and weakness, people sin.[97] It must be realized, of course, that Irenaeus has no notion of biological evolution in the modern sense of the term. He is a keen observer of the human person and finds that the individual progresses from immaturity to maturity.

Saint Augustine, too, does not know the modern concept of evolution. Yet the image he uses to describe original sin makes one think of the evolutionary view of original sin. He speaks of original sin as a *vitium*. The image is medical. It brings to mind the notion of original sin as a hereditary moral disease. The human person contracts it simply by being born of human parents. Augustine's *vitium* imagery is powerful and can easily lead to the impression that there is something intrinsically wrong with human nature, especially human generation and concupiscence. Some authors wish to mark Augustine's view of human nature as pessimistic. Some hold that he identifies original sin and concupiscence. However, one must realize that Augustine is thinking in theological and biblical terms. He is looking at the total situation of humans as *massa damnata*, set at a distance from God through the sin of Adam and Eve. Humans are totally incapable of returning to God's good graces on their own power; they depend on the uplifting hand of God. In their state of distance they are subject to guilt and concupiscence. Concupiscence is itself a sign of their inordinate relationship to creatures and to God.

Augustine's position is certainly not the same as that of modern authors who wish to see original sin in the realm of the evolving person. But his medical images depict original sin as residing in the very flesh and blood of the human person, and it is this aspect that finds its analogy with evolutionary suggestions of today.

5. Society

The sociological interpretation of original sin supposes that the structures of society influence considerably the way in which people think and act. The structures of government, the ways of educating the young, the customs of marriage, the expectations of workers inevitably condition the way in which people define and perceive themselves in society. No person can live beyond the borders of some society; no person is without impressions of some family structure, some political system, some norms of human interaction. Behaviorists like B. F. Skinner even hold that individuals are entirely subject to the influence of societal determinants. The directions and rules of a society mold the way in which individuals think and act. Human freedom is only an illusion.

A less determinist position maintains that society indeed greatly influences the ways in which people think and act, the ways in which they view themselves, but that the influence does not extinguish human freedom (except in certain specified instances). Society at large has a bearing on noble action as well as evil action. Individuals are deeply affected by such influence, perceive it within themselves, and accept it or reject it. Society itself is replete with good models and evil models. Both good and evil press down upon individuals from the very beginning of their existence. Humans are never outside a milieu of good and evil, of virtue and sin, of moral success and failure. There are traditions of evil in a society (e.g., dishonesty and greed) and traditions of good (e.g., heroism, integrity, and self-sacrifice). With life itself human individuals inherit patterns of evil and of good. In their own time they will accept, reject, or adjust these patterns, but they can never be without their influence.

These sociological factors of human existence can clarify the situation of sin. Original sin can be viewed as the evil factors that bear in upon individuals as they live and act in a society. The evil influence is there whether they choose it or not; it antedates their entry upon the sociological scene. People are born into a milieu of sin and failure. Walter

Rauschenbusch says, "Theology has done considerable harm in concentrating the attention of religious minds on the biological transmission of evil. It has diverted our minds from the power of social transmission, from the authority of the social group in justifying, urging, and idealizing wrong, and from the decisive influence of economic profit in the defense and propagation of evil."[98]

The sociological interpretation of original sin explains well a non-voluntary aspect of original sin. It indicates that individuals are influenced externally and internally, in thinking and acting. It makes clear that such an influence goes back in time to the historical origins of human existence on this earth. It allows for the exercise of free will, at least in the normal run of a functioning society.

The theologian who has made considerable use of sociological data to illuminate the dimension of sin in society is Piet Schoonenberg.[99] He postulates a condition of sin which influences people externally and internally. The milieu is pre-personal; it affects people for evil; it even conditions their spiritual relationship with God: the situation is such that divine grace and favor are not passed on. Schoonenberg is not directly concerned with the historical beginning of sin, though he sees the condition of sin as going back in time to the origin of the human society.

Since Schoonenberg's major work appeared before Vatican Council II, it is possible that his writing influenced the thought of the council fathers. In any event the influence of society both for good and evil is clearly cited in the Council's document, "The Church in the Modern World":

> While on the one hand in fulfilling his calling (even his religious calling), man is greatly helped by life in society, on the other hand it cannot be denied that he is often turned away from the good and urged to evil by the social environment in which he lives and in which he is immersed since the day of his birth. Without doubt frequent upheavals in the social order are in part the result of economic, political, and social tensions. But at a deeper level they come from selfishness and pride, two things which contaminate the atmosphere of society as well. As it is, man is prone to evil, but whenever he meets a situation where the effects of sin are to be found, he is exposed to further inducements to sin, which can only be overcome by unflinching effort under the help of grace.[100]

Words like "environment," "immersed," and "atmosphere" are bold expressions of a milieu of sin in which one is born and lives. But there is an even deeper level of perversion: "proneness to evil." The fathers of the council do not define this proneness, but they hold that such an inclination is aggravated by a sphere of sin in society.

The sphere of evil is offset by a sphere of good, a pre-eminent form of which is the Church of Jesus Christ. The Church is the community of believers and a communion in divine and Christic realities. The Church is the place where the good news of salvation is announced; it is the place of the forgiveness of sins; it is the locus of the Holy Spirit and all his gifts;

it is the place of life in Christ; it is the place of faith in the presence of God; it is the place of trust in the Word of God; it is the communion in the love of God; it is the communion of those who accept the approach of the gracious God; it is the place of reconciliation between God and humans; it is the expression of the kingdom; it is the sign of God's favor in Jesus Christ.

The manifold grace of God has indeed become known in the history of Israel and in the Church of Jesus Christ. The grace of God is indeed rich beyond expression, but the Church exists to realize and to utter this grace as much as human language and ritual permit. The Church expresses this grace even in its imperfect condition as a sinful community on the way to perfection in an age to come.

It is acknowledged, of course, that many aspects of grace, as sketched above, are present in the human community outside of the explicit Church of Christ. God's graceful presence is not confined to the Church, to the community of Christian believers. His care and concern extend beyond the explicit borders of the Church to peoples in every part of the world. His presence ensures the power of the Spirit, the forgiveness of sins for people who have the proper moral disposition. Faith and trust in God are expressed in ways of prayer, in ritual, and in societal interaction.[101]

The religious factor of society, expressed in the Church or elsewhere, is of particular concern to us. The religious dimension of a family or of a culture is received and absorbed by individuals of the society. Persons are necessarily affected by the religious principles and rituals that are prevalent in the home or in a culture. Humans receive and absorb the religious factor as they learn language, as they witness the actions of parents and others in society, as they imbibe philosophies of existence. They cannot be unaffected by the way in which members of society profess or deny a religious dimension to human existence.

It is inevitable, therefore, that the community of the Church will affect those who are born of its members or who grow up in direct or indirect association with those who profess membership in the society of the Church. A profession and a practice of Christian faith find their repercussions in the milieu of the family and of the civic community.

The zealous believer is committed to the Christian faith and wishes others to share the benefits of Christian life and thought. He or she ideally will proceed by way of persuasion, ensuring a free acceptance or rejection of the Christian faith. But the believer may also be reluctant to pass on the Christian values; he or she may refuse to do so, or be sluggish in the task. This refusal to hand on Christian values to family or society at large will have an effect on the people who live in that family or society. The people will lack to a certain degree what the believer perceives to be an essential understanding of human existence in this universe.

We may now apply this thought about religion and church to the sociological interpretation of the origin of sin. One factor in the origin of sin is the reluctance to pass on Christian values to others in one's social milieu. It is the refusal to hand on the graceful realities mentioned above. It is the reluctance to hand on the words of God, to show forgiveness, to manifest trust, to teach the kingdom, to represent God's favor, etc. A refusal or reluctance to hand on these Christian realities determines the way in which others will receive them or not receive them. It circumscribes the way in which others come to know and accept the doctrines and practices of the Christian faith. The influence is present apart from the choice of the person who finds himself or herself in this milieu. It is a pre-volitional determination.

Such a refusal is a factor in the origin of sin because it does not provide, or only provides to a certain extent, the kind of word (e.g., of divine graciousness and forgiveness) that could lead one out of despair, that could promote the well-being of self, that could foster loving relationships with others. It is not a direct cause of sin, but it provides the situation in which moral failure easily becomes a reality.

What is at issue here is the requirement of humans to foster a milieu in which others can grow up and live in a maximum amount of well-being and encouragement. What is at issue also is the idea that the grace of God is enfleshed in very concrete communities, that it is possible to manifest these graces and to inherit them, and that it is possible to squander them, refusing to bequeath them to others in a milieu.

The Church as a society influences individuals for good and evil. We confess in the creed that the Church is "one, holy, catholic, and apostolic." The Church is holy because it is united to Jesus Christ and lives in the power of the Holy Spirit. It is an expression of the kingdom of Christ and is directed to the eschatological goal of union with God. But it is also a matter of faith that the Church has not yet arrived at its goal; it is still a pilgrim church, a community on the way to perfection. It is not perfect in the present time but seeks perfection in a time to come. This means that the Church as it exists now exhibits a dimension of sin. Vatican II refrained from the bold statement that the Church is sinful, but it did recognize that there are sinners in the Church: "The Church, however, clasping sinners to her bosom, at once holy and always in need of purification, follows constantly the path of penance and renewal."[102] Since sinners are in the Church and constitute the Church, it is legitimate to say that the Church itself is sinful. The Church has been known to misuse power, to support the oppression of minorities (e.g., of blacks and of Jews) within so-called Christian countries.

The only point we wish to make here is that the sinful aspects of the Church constitute part of the larger society in which a person is born and develops. The Church not only conditions a person for good but also, perhaps only in a limited way, for evil. In speaking about the evil influence of a society, we cannot neglect the influence of the society or the Church. Its way of dealing with people—its way of limiting freedom, dominating thoughts and actions—situates them and contributes in its own fashion to the sinful dimension which bears in upon persons in society.

In sum, society is the human context in which one is born, lives, and dies. It influences a person for good and for evil. A person is never born into a neutral situation where there is complete autonomy and where one would be free of the good or bad suggestions of others. Insofar as society forces a person into a position of failure, he or she is not responsible, for complete determination eliminates freedom and responsibility.

But society can determine action to a great extent. Determination in the direction of evil and failure conditions a person to the extent that evil is at hand, that moral failure is a possibility, that a fall into sin is understandable. The tradition of sin in society from the very beginning of the human race causes a great deal of evil to mount up in the world. This evil is ever pressing down on individuals, ever suggesting a devious path, ever depriving a person of sound vision and insight. It is the dimension of sin in society that constitutes a factor in the origin of sin. It is not the whole cause of sin, but it certainly provides a situation in which sin is possible and easily becomes embodied in action.

6. Human Psyche

Do the psychological dynamics of the human person help to explain the origin and condition of sin? Can the situation of sin be defined in psychological terms? Must the origin of sin be sought in the history of the human psyche?

It is well known that Sigmund Freud (1856-1939) proposes to explain the character of original sin in terms of the Oedipus complex. The Oedipus complex concerns the desire of the son to possess his mother and to subdue his father. Freud sees this dynamic at work in the primitive history of humankind. He holds that there was a primitive murder; the sons rose up and killed their father. Then they ate his body in a kind of sacrificial meal; and to avoid a series of murders they made a pact not to kill each other. The murder of the father portrays the classic opposition between father and son (or sons), and the meal indicates their wish to assimilate his power and position. The pact is firmly in place, but the guilt of the original act remains. The original state of humans, therefore, is not one of innocence and peace but one of evil impulses.

Freud then endeavors to explain the "illusion" of religion. It is an attempt to solve the murder of the father and the guilt that proceeds from this act. Humankind remembers the primitive act and seeks reconciliation.

Reconciliation is the goal of religious doctrine and practices; Christ's sacrifice and the sacrificial meal are means of effecting the reconciliation.

While we cannot accept Freud's mythic explanation of the origin of religion and of original sin, we must acknowledge the fruitfulness of his analysis of the human psyche. A principle of Freud's understanding of the human psyche is "that we can have strivings and feelings and wishes which motivate our actions and yet of which we have no awareness."[103]

His analysis of narcissism is especially helpful in a modern understanding of original sin. Narcissism is characteristic of the human psyche. It is a drive that stems from self and is directed to self. The narcissistic drive makes its appearance in infancy and early childhood. Freud identifies these strivings as social (incestual, etc.).[104] The infant centers its world on itself—its needs for food, warmth, and affection. There is a libido, a power and energy directed toward the seeking of vital and sexual needs. The child, however, meets with opposition in the form of competition and prohibitions; not everything is available and allowed; e.g., incest is forbidden. The energy of the libido is then diverted to acceptable objects, to works of culture, and to other persons.

There is a continual interplay between the drives of the libido and the understanding of the conscious ego. The adult person is always in danger of reverting to the narcissism of childhood. Dreams and neuroses are the signs that, when analyzed properly, provide an understanding of the energies and struggles. The self can become divided, alienated from its true self.

Freud's discussion of narcissism within the broader context of psychic spheres (unconscious, pre-conscious, conscious; id, ego, super-ego; eros, thanatos) can elucidate the condition of sin. Narcissistic drives provide the possibility of moral evil in the form of selfishness and greed. Human individuals grow up with narcissistic drives that are more or less evident throughout their life. They perceive the division within themselves, the drive toward self-interests, egoistic goals, isolation, and alienation from others. While these egoistic drives are understandable and inevitable, they are not beyond the realm of freedom and moral activity. One can freely acknowledge and accept narcissistic goals; one can decide to foster the egoistic drives to the exclusion of self-sacrificial endeavors and to the detriment of the needs and interests of other persons.

Sharon MacIsaac puts the self-dividedness in terms of "concupiscence," a term that through the centuries has carried much of the burden of the theology of original sin. She says that concupiscence "describes a situation which derives from the conscious/unconscious dualism in man."[105] There is a tension between the dynamic unconscious and the mental functions of the human person. In response to the tension there is a struggle for integration, especially of the sexual instincts: an integration of narcissistic and altruistic drives, an integration of love and hate.[106]

The psychological interpretation of original sin is not the total understanding of the situation of sin. But it catches significant aspects of the condition of sin. It indicates that there are pre-personal and pre-conscious data that must be taken into account when one is doing a theology of sin. The psychological drives, while they are present for the well-being and preservation of life, can disrupt the human psyche. The psychological drives indicate that there is a pre-determined division in the very heart of the human person. But it is a division, an alienation, that to some extent can be overcome in the course of one's life. There is a range of human freedom that can attend to the signs of disintegration. There is a range of human freedom that can work to overcome self-dividedness and the alienation from others.

7. Economics

Many writers and speakers decry the extravagances of the modern world of economics and technology. Opinions range from an outright denunciation of almost all technological advances to a mild opposition to selective achievements of technology. There is frequent outcry against the waste and the destruction that accompany the creation of new weapons systems. Many say that an undue proportion of the earth's resources is spent on the development of arms and protective devices.

Others declaim against the economic systems of countries, especially capitalist countries. They cite the teachings of Karl Marx (1818-1883), who described the condition of workers in most industries of the 19th century as a state of alienation. He believed that because of the capitalist system workers become alienated from their work. They offer their labor but do not receive a fair share of the produce. This alienation of the workers from the product of their labors, according to Marx, is the root of all evil in society.[107] Because of this evil the rich become richer and the poor become poorer.

The communist countries today follow rather widely divergent versions of Marx's teaching. It is to be noted that, while economic conditions improved for many people in these countries, the problem of alienation is not appreciably solved. Workers are still alienated from the products of their labors, and they certainly do not receive an equal share of them. The myth of the classless society and of an earthly paradise has not reached fruition. Moreover, the waste due to technology and war production continues apace in these countries.

The economic plight of many workers today, especially those in the third world, is evidence of a basic alienation that exists in most societies today. The economic situation may be regarded as the root cause of ills for many societies. In some societies where the workers are alienated from their land and work, there is a great chasm between the rich and the poor, there is unequal access to the fruits of the earth, there is exploitation of the land on the part of the rich, there is a tie between the rich and the governments (local and foreign), there is waste of the resources of the land.

This is not the place to cite the economic ills of practically every country of the world. What is important to note is the continuing alienation that exists between the worker and the fruit of his or her labor. The alienation may be regarded as an indication of a basic sin in society. This alienation is pre-personal in the sense that people find themselves born into this situation. It affects them as they grow up in society. It is the kind of alienation that they can oppose, or accept and foster.

In the context of our discussion of original sin, the alienation and the extravagances of the technological society can be regarded as a split that occurs in persons and in society at large. It is the split that characterizes original sin, the division in self and society. It is a split that a people inherit, oppose, or foster. It affects every moment of life and remains to some extent in every person and society.

8. Human Volition

The capacity to will, to make decisions, and to pursue the intention of the heart is a human benefit of the highest proportions. Human persons are not limited to the mechanical and deterministic; they willingly incline their energies in the direction of human endeavors, such as intellectual designs, crafts, art, etc. Volition allows human persons to reach out to change their immediate environment and to create new modes of existence. But as the will reaches out, it is capable of pursuing both the good and the evil.

a. Volitional Evil

The immediate condition of sin is the human capacity for willing. Without the factor of volition, without the ability to choose, there can be no accountability, no responsibility, and no moral failure. The volitional dimension of the human person provides the very possibility of moral good and moral evil.

Scripture designates the human heart as a source of evil. In biblical language the heart is the seat of understanding, desire, and affection. The heart is summoned to fix its love on the Word of God and the well-being of others. But it is often bent on evil, inclined toward evil from the beginning of life: "Indeed, in guilt was I born, and in sin my mother conceived me; behold, you are pleased with sincerity of heart, and in my inmost being you teach me wisdom" (Ps 51:7-8). The psalmist does not mean that human generation and motherhood are sinful but that one is directed toward evil from the very first moment of existence.

The story of the flood is introduced with the complaint that every heart is wicked: "When the Lord saw how great was man's wickedness on earth, and how no desire that his heart conceived was ever anything but evil, he regretted that he had made man on the earth, and his heart was grieved" (Gen 6:5-6). The prophets, too, viewed the heart as the source of evil: "More tortuous than all else is the human heart, beyond remedy; who can understand it?" (Jer 17:9; cf. Isa 29:13-14)

The same evaluation of the heart or mind is included in the teachings of Jesus: "From the mind stem evil designs—murder, adulterous conduct, fornication, stealing, false witness, blasphemy. These are the things that make a man impure. As for eating with unwashed hands—that makes no man impure" (Matt 15:19-20). Evil activity is formed first in the heart of the human person; he or she ponders evil and from this inner deliberation comes what is truly and morally devious.

The goodness of the Mosaic Law is axiomatic for Paul. But he finds another law in his body, a power of sin and an inclination to evil. He depicts the classical dilemma, the struggles between the desires of the will and the forces of sin: "I do not do what I want to do but what I hate. When I act against my own will, by that very fact I agree that the law is good. This indicates that it is not I who do it but sin which resides in me. I know that no good dwells in me, that is, in my flesh; the desire to do right is there but not the power" (Rom 7:15-18). Paul experiences the strength of sin in his own person; he has a will to do the good but the power of sin overwhelms him and he pursues the unintended evil. Only the power of God can assist him. What is important to notice is that Paul wills the good, has a desire for the good. The desire to effect the good remains, but the good can be accomplished only through the powerful and liberating grace of God.[108]

The Scriptures and Church tradition teach that evil exists in every heart. Exceptions are Jesus and Mary, whom tradition regards as divinely freed from the dividedness of heart that results in moral failure. Other humans, however, experience the dividedness of an evil heart. Good and evil coexist in the same heart, in the same inner sphere of thinking and willing. A dimension of evil is present before the human person reaches the age of decision. Evil is there in the form of the many adverse determinisms that converge upon the person as he or she enters the world. The evil becomes moral evil when the person freely acknowledges the devious situation, accepts it, consents to it, and expresses it in action. The heart inclined toward evil becomes morally devious when it chooses to follow the inclination.

Scripture prefers the imagery of the heart. But philosophers and religious thinkers depict the volitional capacity of the human person in a great variety of terms and images. Some speak of a separate faculty of willing, parallel and relative to the faculty of intellect. Others exalt the power of the will to the point of identifying it as the directive and creative force of the whole world. Still others see it as the source of motivation and evaluation.

The volitional power is understood here as the inner dynamism of the person toward self, others, and the world at large. It is the inner power to act or to refuse to act, to pursue a goal or to refuse to pursue a goal. It is a directive movement from within the person to accomplish a task. It is a conscious and willful movement of the person in the projection of a possible work or course of action and in the decision to accomplish it. Mortimer Adler defines human freedom in these terms: "A man is free who has in himself the ability or power whereby he can make what he does his own action and what he achieves his own property."[109] The volitional activity of the person sets in operation a movement that changes the world of self and the world of others. The dynamism of the will creates conditions of well-being or of harm for others. It expresses itself in works that either enhance or destroy the surrounding world of nature and culture.

The power of volition is directed toward those actions that are perceived as possible of execution. Persons may indeed *wish* to undertake some kinds of activities, but they do not have the physical capacity to initiate them (e.g., to fly by waving one's arms). The power of volition is directed to the possible, but even within the realm of the possible the person is not constrained to choose everything. Persons do not have to pursue all their capabilities. They may activate only a few. They have the freedom, at least to a limited degree, to choose or not to choose activation of these capabilities.

The volitional capacity of the human person stands at a crucial juncture of existence. Intelligent, conscious, and capable, the human person stands at the crossroads of a space-time horizon. The vast universe lies open before it—the universe of the galaxies, the universe of the infra-human sphere of the cosmos. At a particular juncture in this universe the human person is called upon to make a decision. As the person makes the decision, he or she is influenced by the whole weight of the evolving universe: the gropings of evolution for billions of years, the decisions of ancestors, the inherited gifts of intellect and charm. An infinite number of factors come to a point in the eruption of freedom. The eruption is like a bubble that finally finds its way to the surface of fathoms of water.

    b. Volition and Finitude

The will has objective limits. The range of its freedom is limited, for the will has to work with the possibilities at hand, with the polarity of actuality and possibility. In the words of Langdon Gilkey, which recall those of Paul Tillich: "The fundamental ontological structure of finite being in history is the polarity of destiny and freedom."[110] The relationship between freedom (which entails the domination of nature by a spiritual being) and finiteness (which entails being part of nature) is sometimes branded as contradictory. Reinhold Niebuhr cites Albrecht Ritschl to this effect, and, while Niebuhr agrees with this estimation of the relationship, he adds that the Bible really subordinates the problem of finiteness to the problem of sin and that it regards the contradiction as an occasion of sin, not as a cause of sin.[111]

The will's field of choice is limited to the actual living situation in which a person finds himself or herself. The available courses of action are determined by the complex of circumstances that are present at the moment of decision. The finite complex of circumstances is the very field of human freedom.

Life is accidental and chancy. It depends on many accidental happenings of the past: the vagaries of an evolving cosmos and the free decisions of millions of other persons who have shaped the present world. The evolutionary movements of life and the free choices of countless individuals of the past have brought the individual of the present to the point where only select choices are available to him or her. For example, the field of choice is limited by the century or decade in which one lives. A scientist of the nineteenth century could not engage in the kind of space exploration that is available to scientists today. He or she was confined to the progress that was achieved in the last century. A person living in the jungles of Brazil today does not readily have the opportunity to study astronomy. A person growing up in a family circle of wise but illiterate parents is not likely to imbibe a love for the classics of Greek literature. A choice for the moral good is narrow for the person born into a family where graft and deception are a way of business.

The finitude of the will, therefore, involves the accidental combinations and circumscriptions of millions and billions of years; it involves the choices of innumerable persons who lived before the present moment and who have determined the individual's current field of choice. It is impossible for the individual to trace all the factors that make up a particular field of choice. If a person would attempt to do this before making a decision, he or she would be stymied. The factors are always beyond exhaustive and minute examination. But people continue to make choices; they make choices with the actual, though limited, perception of the circumstances.

The finitude of the will is limited in regard to the future. The free individual of today can determine to some extent the immediate future; but his or her influence is limited, and it is subject to the "correction" of later cosmic developments and to the decisions of future free agents. Moreover, the future ramifications of the free choice are not perceived. It is possible, of course, to foresee many immediate consequences of a particular course of action. But no one can see all the results of a decision, for no one can predict the future of the cosmic development nor the free decisions of subsequent generations.

The dynamism of the will is limited by the many contingencies of a particular time and place. These are the givens of an historical moment of decision. It must be recognized, however, that the givens come not only from without the person but also from within. One's potentialities are provided by many circumstances: heredity, education, strength of will, etc. There is a sense in which a person develops his or her own givens; a person receives an initial gift of life, even though limited, and shapes this gift, develops it, and augments it. The particular givens are limitations, but they are open to dynamic development.

Since finitude characterizes the human capacity of will, it is foolhardy to neglect real limitations. It is not only foolhardy but also sinful, at least in the estimation of many theologians. It is a sin of pride to attempt to go beyond human limits, specifically beyond one's own potentialities. It is an attempt to be or to do what one is not. It is a refusal to recognize one's own existential possibilities. And this is an aspect of pride. "His sin is never the mere ignorance of his ignorance. It is always partly an effort to obscure his blindness by overestimating the degree of his sight and to obscure his insecurity by stretching his power beyond its limits."[112]

Within the circle of possibilities available to the human person, the objects of need are of the first order. One needs air to breathe; one needs warmth and food; one needs to preserve life both in oneself and in the species; one needs affection. These objects of need can become volitional in the sense that the will positively and freely chooses to pursue them. One can also choose not to pursue them, even to reject them. Surely one cannot follow this mode of action very long, in particular with regard to air, food, and warmth. But people have been known to initiate a hunger strike to underscore a religious or political point. People have been known to give up sexual involvement for a time or for life in the pursuit of religious and cultural goals. People have been known to give up life itself in suicide or in sacrifice to a cause. The point to be made here is that human needs are numerous, and the will is capable of governing these, at least to some extent. It can govern the time and the quality of their fulfillment—always within the limited possibilities available to the person.

Needs, however, are not the same as desires. One may desire needs, but one may also desire objects beyond one's needs. This is not to say that one's desires must always be limited to basic needs. Obviously a person may desire objects of art and culture which surpass the fundamental needs of living. But one can also be deceived by one's desires. One can desire the fulfillment of needs in a way that is harmful to self and others. One can overeat. One can steal food from the hungry. One can force oneself upon another affectionately and sexually. The fulfillment of one's basic needs is an occasion to engage in an evil will and a wrong action. In other words, the very fact that humans are such that they are required to fulfill certain needs within limited circumstances already sets up the occasion for an evil pursuit of these needs.

The fulfillment of one's basic needs has another built-in danger: the possibility of delusion in the realm of imagination. The basic needs of the human person are represented to the conscious ego in the form of imagination (imagination of the object and of the way in which it satisfies). The imagination can be more or less representative of the actual need; it can exaggerate the need; it can send the will in a direction that is harmful to self or to others. Paul Ricoeur says that imagination can make the object fascinating and charming: ". . . imagination is *in addition* a privileged point of entry of what in subsequent works we shall call the fault. . . . The charm of imagination, the magic power of absence, thus seems to us to go back to a guilty consciousness, a consciousness which has already given in to temptation."[113] "Need is bewildered, misled about its own real demands. All human civilization, from its economy to its sciences and its arts, is marked by this trait of discontent and frenzy."[114] Needs, therefore, while they are good and wholesome in themselves, are part of human existence. Needs are finite, pre-personal and pre-volitional in the sense that they are demands of the human condition, though they are also the objects of will and desire. The point to be made, however, is that the very existence of needs makes it possible for a person to fail freely in their fulfillment.

The risk characteristic of willing is another aspect of its finitude. Willing is always a risk. A person must decide without having an exact knowledge of all the circumstances that brought him or her to a point of decision. A person decides without having an accurate knowledge of the consequences of an action. A person decides without knowing precisely whether a decision will serve one's development or not. A free decision can result in good or evil for oneself and others; in fact, it can result in both good and evil for oneself and others. One risks oneself in free decision. The risk is that the decision could prove harmful to self and others.

Relation is another aspect of willing's finitude. Both sin and freedom are always relational. Just as freedom is freedom for others, freedom for God, and freedom for self, so also is sin a misuse of freedom for others, for God and for self. Sin is freedom that does not serve the well-being of self and of others. Sin corrupts relationships. Sin appears to be in the best interests of self, since it is basically a selfish turning in upon self. It does not go out to God and to others. It does not seek their good and exaltation. Every form of sin, from self-adulation to institutional violence, harms life's relationships.

How much of this harm stems from the relational structure of human life? An individual must exist in a network of relationships: parents, friends, fellow workers, neighbors, earth, cosmos. An individual must carve out a personal existence in this complex of relationships. It is the task of the individual freely to create a life, freely to pursue the opportunities of one's existence, freely to develop one's potentialities. But the task of one individual impinges on the lives of others. One's action is like the movement of waves produced by a stone thrown in a pool of water; the waves go out from a point and reach far and wide. One's actions touch many other persons and their legitimate desires to develop themselves. The ideal is to pattern one's self-development to the requirements of innumerable relationships.

B. F. Skinner speaks of a conflict of interests. He promotes behavior modification through positive reward and reinforcement. While he allows for the existence of planners in a society, he ultimately holds that humans are influenced by and respond to an environment. "Each of us has interests which conflict with the interests of everybody else. That's our original sin, and it can't be helped. Now, 'everybody else' we call 'society.' It's a powerful opponent, and it always wins."[115]

Here we can speak of conflict in the task of self-development. Self-development ought to be pursued, not to the detriment of others, but to the enhancement of others. One's self-development is precisely the assistance and exaltation of others. Self-development is not, in this situation, at the expense of the others but in relation to their well-being.

But there is opportunity for moral failure precisely in this process of self-development as it relates to self, to others, and to God. Self-development is the place where one has the opportunity to fail self and others. One could develop only one aspect of self (e.g., one's scientific knowledge) to the detriment of other aspects (e.g., one's affective relationships to wife or husband, children, and friends). One could develop one's own interests to the point of tyrannizing others. One could develop one's sense of importance to the exclusion of the God of the universe.

Relationships—the place of a person's call to development and the very means of development—are the occasions of moral failure. It is not just that a person lacks knowledge, that it is impossible to consider all the factors of one's actions in their relation to others, to self, and to God. The truth is that a person cannot do anything about the fact of relationships: he or she must develop in relation to others; relationships can lead to sin and failure. Neither relationships nor a failure in them can be wished away. Does this mean that sin (failure in relationships) is necessary? Not free? If it is not free, it is not sin. But here we are looking for the very structures of human existence which inevitably lead to sin. One of these structures is the need to develop in society, to grow in relation to others, to mature in the finitude of relationships.

c. Freedom and Necessity

Necessity and choice characterize human life. Much of life is beyond willful determination; it is a given, a patrimony, a structure which is present before persons set out to determine a direction for themselves. But people do determine themselves, at least within a limited range of possibilities. Assumed here is the existence of a human capacity to deliberate, to choose, to consent, to act, and to refuse to act. Paul Ricoeur offers a triadic interpretation of the act of the will: "To say, 'I will' means first 'I decide,' secondly 'I move my body,' thirdly 'I consent.'"[116] Or again, "To decide means first of all to project a practical possibility of an action which depends on me, secondly to impute myself as the author responsible for the project, and finally to motivate my project by reasons and variables which 'historialize' values capable of justifying them."[117] Freedom is a capacity to choose values; it is a volitional power that selects what is good for the well-being of the person; it is a volitional dynamism that can choose what is harmful for self and for others.[118]

The idea that there is both choice and given structures (necessity and chance) is ancient. Plato recognizes this duality in *The Republic*: in the Myth of Er, the souls who are about to begin a new round of earthly life are required to select their own destiny among the choices that are available: "Let him to whom the first lot falls choose first a life to which he will be bound of necessity. But Virtue owns no master: as a man honours or dishonours her, so shall he have more of her or less. The blame is his who chooses; Heaven is blameless." So spoke the interpreter for Lachesis, the daughter of Necessity.[119]

The sacred Scriptures assume both a world of creation and a realm of freedom. The invitation to covenant, to call to discipleship, the command to obey, the threat of punishment, the promise of reward—these and other features of the sacred writings are without sense unless humans are free to choose good and evil. The myth of paradise and the fall presupposes the responsibility of the first couple. The story of the murder of Abel manifests the freedom and accountability of Adam's descendants. The Lord said to Cain: "Why are you so resentful and crestfallen? If you do well, you can hold up your head; but if not, sin is a demon lurking at the door: his urge is toward you, yet you can be his master" (Gen 4:6-7). The human person is responsible for his or her actions, even when tempted by outside forces.

It is well known that the Fathers of the Church were obliged to defend human freedom against various forms of determinism. The Greek Fathers in particular defended human freedom against the determinist positions of the gnostics and the Manichaeans, as well as against a tradition of divine fate that generally characterized the Greek myths. The Latin Fathers were also concerned about personal responsibility. Saint Augustine, for instance, took up the subject early in his writing career. He spoke very boldly about the freedom of the will in the face of Manichaean denials (denials which he understood very well from his own Manichaean days). Later, Augustine found himself battling with Pelagians, who overstressed the liberty of the human will. He then strove to manifest to them that, while the divinely created human will is free, it is bound by Adam's sin and needs the saving power of God if it is to find release for eternal life: "Our will, however, is always free, but it is not always good. For it is either free from justice when it serves sin, and then it is evil; or it is free from sin when it serves justice, and then it is good."[120]

Theology has always maintained as a necessary datum that moral evil of any kind ultimately depends on the freedom of the will. No moral evil, no moral failure, no personal responsibility can exist without the dimension of freedom. Where there is freedom, there is the possibility of moral good and evil; where there is no freedom, there is no possibility of moral good and evil.

Freedom is present in the volitional dynamism of the human person. But it is not absolute freedom. It is a freedom that abides in the midst of limited possibilities. In the words of Paul Ricoeur, "a decision is never more than an islet of clarity in an obscure, moving sea of unknown potentialities."[121] The will finds itself in the center of a huge array of possibilities and necessities. Most of life is a given, an already-there before the will comes to the point of free decision. The givens of cosmic evolution, psychological development (both conscious and unconscious), and culture confront the individual who is brought to the point of freedom.

The given factors of life appear both threatening and challenging. They threaten to overwhelm the individual, to carry him or her along an irresistible stream of power and energy. It seems impossible to carve out a free existence in this vast movement of force and mass. It is clear that one individual can get lost in a vast universe that he or she did not create. The great mass of the universe is there without one's willing, without one's creation. But there is nevertheless the moment of freedom, the volitional effort that moves a tiny portion of the given universe. The moment of choice becomes "The peak of previous growth and . . . the surge of novelty."[122] It is the possibility to move a portion of the given world that is a challenge and a wonder. The given world is there for support of life, for development, and for the works of love and beauty.

An aspect of free will, therefore, is the consent to necessity. It is an acceptance of the way in which the universe exists, a yielding to the forces over which the individual has no control. Consent is going along with the forces of the cosmos. But it is also a rising to the challenge of the universe in order to create what one is able to fashion in the midst of the world. The consent can be all too easy if one chooses to drift along with the forces of the universe. The consent can be angry if one only wishes to curse the powers and givens of the universe. The will can choose whether to rage or to drift or to create. The volitional dynamism of the human person can be directed to any of these. It can create a space for itself in the midst of necessity.

Another aspect of free will is the consent to the many challenges that present themselves to the person in his or her concrete existence. The givens of life are the opportunities and suggestions that are provided by human life. Ricoeur speaks of reflective choice that "follows from some non-reflective movement, some inchoate act, tendency or inclination which deserves the name of spontaneous will or natural freedom."[123] From one standpoint the inclinations and tendencies can be seen as dimensions of the necessary in one's human existence; from another they can be viewed as proximate incentives to free choice. They precede immediately the reflective choice of free will.

It is possible, of course, that the givens of the universe press in on the human person and extinguish free choice. Their power and effectiveness can be so great that they render human responsibility impossible. On the other hand, they may situate the human person only to a certain extent, only to the point of lessening, but not to the point of annihilating freedom. The measure of responsibility and freedom can be sensed to some extent by the individual, but an exact assessment cannot be determined by the individual or by others.

Determinists hold that the conjunction of all these factors account for any course of action without remainder. They maintain that if one could measure all the circumstantial factors that bear upon an event of "decision," one would ascertain that they provide sufficient reason for the action. The multiple factors involved in the action would totally account for its appearance.

A theology of sin, however, maintains that precisely in the face of all these factors a range of free will remains. The external and internal influences bring many modes of action to the point of possibility; they motivate the person and even incline the will toward a particular decision; but they do not pre-determine any one mode of action. There is the point of freedom that ultimately erupts and gives direction to a movement of thought or action.

Human volition lies at the core of moral good and evil. Human volition is limited and set about by many necessities but it retains a dimension of freedom. Freedom, even limited freedom, with all its risks and relationships exists as the ultimate reason for moral good and evil. Its finitude and limitations, its tendency to overstep bounds of needs and desires, its inclination to overstress self to the detriment of others—these provide the disposition that makes moral failure possible.

9. Summary of Chapter I

Chapter I has given us a fairly diverse and comprehensive view of the various attempts to explain the origin of sin in the world. Some of the attempts are quite unacceptable, for example, the myths that place the origin of sin in God either by making the divine being the direct cause of all evil in the world or by citing him as the author of an evil creation. The doctrine of the Church proclaims both the sacred activity of God and the goodness of creation; it rejects the idea that the corporeal in itself is evil. While the Bible and Christian tradition cite the influence of demonic forces, they are quite clear that ultimately humans are not coerced to follow demonic promptings.

Saint Augustine notes that creation is made from nothingness, and this condition makes it possible for humans to turn away from God. There is a real deficiency in their condition when humans turn away from the God for whom they were made.

Saint Thomas continues with the notion of evil as privation, the lack of something that should be present. Both he and Saint Augustine teach that the present situation of humans is a privation of the original relationship with God in the Garden of Eden. After the fall of Adam and Eve, humans inherit a deficient situation.

The Augustinian-Thomistic explanation of original sin, based as it is on acceptance of an historical fall, is regarded as deficient by many modern authors. What is valid, however, is the concept of an inherited situation which affects the choices of humans today.

The more philosophical attempts of Hegel and Tillich tend to view too negatively the actual state of created beings in this world. Particular beings existing at a distance from Spirit are evil (Hegel), or creation itself as it exists in this world is already a fall (Tillich). While these suggestions stress the important concepts of alienation and estrangement, they do not safeguard sufficiently the goodness of created existents. Still they point up well the distance from God as the very possibility of voluntary self-centeredness and sin.

Ricoeur's image of the fault, exemplified in the split between the voluntary and the involuntary, safeguards the concept of goodness in creation and points up the underlying dividedness that characterizes human existence.

The evolutionary view of humans must be taken into consideration in any study of evil and sin. It seems clear that humans have come through a long struggle to secure a life on this planet. There have been and are violent struggles for food and territory, life and posterity. While the evolutionary drive that is still present in the human community is not sufficient and adequate of itself to explain moral evil, it must be regarded as a significant force, contending with which humans freely choose evil, especially the evil of harmful violence.

Akin to the evolutionary background of sin is the influence of society. Humans are influenced by the sinful dimensions of society. There is a "sinsphere" in which everyone is born and lives out his or her life. Again, while society is not the ultimate or only backdrop of moral evil, it surely must be taken into account when listing the "reasons" for moral failure. Humans choose evil in the midst of a society where sin is prevalent.

It should be clear that the human person does not choose moral evil in a neutral situation. The human will is only a limited power, easily turned in upon itself and prone to self-deception. Furthermore, its moment of choice takes place against the horizon of a history of sin, a societal dimension of failure, and an evolutionary struggle. The human will finds itself pulled and tugged in many directions, but ultimately it must make a decision in spite of its weaknesses and limitations. The human will is hemmed in by its many historical, biological, and created conditions; but in the final analysis it must choose to augment its separation from the good in others (disunity), or it must foster its communion with others (community).

Footnotes

Bible quotations are from *The New American Bible*. New York: P.J. Kenedy & Sons, 1970.

CHAPTER 1

[1]Kenneth Burke, "On the First Three Chapters of Genesis," *Symbolism in Religion and Literature,* ed. Rollo May (New York: George Braziller, 1960), p. 136.

[2]See G. C. Berkouwer, *Sin* (Grand Rapids: Eerdmans, 1971), p. 17.

[3]Paul Ricoeur, *The Symbolism of Evil* (New York: Harper & Row, 1967), p. 243.

[4]See, e.g., Carlos Mesters, *Eden: Golden Age or Goad to Action?* (Maryknoll, N.Y.: Orbis Books, 1974).

[5]See P. Ricoeur, *The Symbolism of Evil*, pp. 175-183; J. B. Pritchard (ed.), *The Ancient Near East. An Anthology of Texts and Pictures* (Princeton, N.J.: Princeton University Press, 1958), p. 37; T. Jacobsen, *The Treasures of Darkness. A History of Mesopotamian Religion* (New Haven: Yale University Press, 1976), p. 181.

[6]See M. Noth: "Pharaoh is thus as much a tool of the divine action on the one side, by acting with it without realizing this while following the dictates of his will (cf. Rom. 9.17), as is Moses on the other; all this happens so that many wonderful

signs may take place in Egypt (10.1f.; 11.9)." *Exodus. A Commentary* (Philadelphia: The Westminster Press, 1962), p. 68. Cf. B. Childs: "Hardening was the vocabulary used by the biblical writers to describe the resistance which prevented the signs from achieving their assigned task." *The Book of Exodus. A Critical Theological Commentary* (Philadelphia: The Westminster Press, 1974), p. 174. R. Wilson holds that the J, E, and P accounts of the plagues manifest various uses of the hardening motif. The motif functions as a literary device to hold the accounts of the plagues together, reveals theologically the control that God has of the situation, and refers to the theme of the holy war (God's destruction of Israel's foes); see "The Hardening of Pharaoh's Heart," *Catholic Biblical Quarterly,* 41 (1979), pp. 18-26.

[7]Cf. Isa 45:7: "I form the light, and create the darkness, I make well-being and create woe; I, the Lord, do all these things."

[8]See also this passage from the later wisdom literature: "Good and evil, life and death, poverty and riches, are from the Lord" (Sir 11:14).

[9]Hans Jonas, *The Gnostic Religion* (Boston: Beacon Press, 1963), pp. 62-63.

[10]Note also the Upanishads of Hinduism where one cause of evil is ascribed to the conflict between gods and demons; see John Bowker, *Problems of Suffering in Religions of the World* (Cambridge: Cambridge University Press, 1970), p. 210.

[11]See James M. Robinson, *The Nag Hammadi Library in English* (New York: Harper & Row, 1977), pp. 99-116.

[12]p. 107.

[13]Jes P. Asmussen, *Manichaean Literature.* Representative Texts Chiefly from Middle Persian and Parthian Writings, selected, introduced, and partly translated by Jes P. Asmussen (Delmar, New York: Scholars' Facsimiles and Reprints, 1975), p. 129.

[14]See J. P. Asmussen, *Manichaean Literature,* p. 137. For other accounts of Manichaeism see H. Jonas, *The Gnostic Religion,* Chapter 9; J. Ries, "Manichaeism," *New Catholic Encyclopedia,* Vol. 9 (New York: McGraw-Hill, 1967), pp. 153-160.

[15]See Mircea Eliade, *The Myth of the Eternal Return* (New York: Pantheon Books, 1954), pp. 130-137.

[16]Canon 1, *Enchiridion Symbolorum Definitionum et Declarationum de rebus Fidei et Morum,* eds. H. Denzinger-A. Schönmetzer, editio XXXIII (Barcelona: Herder, 1965) no. 800. (Hereafter cited as DS.)

[17]Walter Kasper, *Jesus the Christ* (New York: Paulist Press, 1976), p. 73.

[18]Canon 1, DS no. 800.

[19]Peter Schoonenberg, S.J., *God's World in the Making* (Pittsburgh, Pa.: Duquesne University Press, 1964), p. 9, note 16.

[20]*Letter to Demetrias,* Chap. 8. J. Migne, *Patrologiae cursus completus. Series Latina* (Paris 1844ff), 30, 23. (Hereafter cited as PL.)

[21]See John Ferguson, *Pelagius. An Historical and Theological Study* (Cambridge: W. Heffer and Sons, 1956), p. 51.

[22]*On the Possibility of not Sinning,* IV (PL Sup. Vol. 1, 1461).

[23]*Vitium* means basically a defect or blemish of the body.

[24]*The City of God,* Bk. 12, 1. *Corpus Scriptorum Ecclesiasticorum Latinorum* (Vienna: C. Gerold's Son, 1866ff) 40, Vol. 1, 568. (Hereafter cited as CSEL.)

[25]*Ibid.,* Bk. 12, 6 (CSEL 40, Vol. 1, 575).

[26]*Ibid.,* Bk. 12, 7 (CSEL 40, Vol. 1, 577).

[27]See Oliver O'Donovan's conclusions about self-love in Augustine: "We have distinguished different evaluative tones which the phrase [self-love] may carry: an unfavorable tone, with which it represents the root of all sin and rebellion

against God; a neutral tone, to represent the natural condition either of man's animal or of his rational nature; a favorable tone, to represent man's discovery of his true welfare in God." *The Problem of Self-Love in Saint Augustine* (New Haven: Yale University Press, 1980), p. 137.

[28]Bk. 7, 16 (CSEL 33, 161). Cf. Sir 10:12.

[29]*The City of God*, Bk. 14, 13 (CSEL 40, Vol. 2, 31).

[30]*Ibid.*

[31]*The City of God*, Bk. 13, 14 (CSEL 40, Vol. 1, 632).

[32]*The City of God*, Bk. 13, 23 (CSEL 40, Vol. 1, 649).

[33]*On Various Questions to Simplician*, I, 16 (PL 40, 121).

[34]*On Marriage and Concupiscence*, Bk. 2, 15 (CSEL 42, 266-267).

[35]*The Grace of Christ and Original Sin*, Chap. 32, 37 (CSEL 42, 196).

[36]The basic image of *reatus* is legal; the *reus* is the one legally accused in court.

[37]*On Marriage and Concupiscence*, Bk. 1, Chap. 23 (CSEL 42, 237-238).

[38]Bk. 1, Chap. 25 (CSEL 42, 240).

[39]*Against Two Letters of the Pelagians*, Bk. I, II, 5 (CSEL 60, 425-426).

[40]*On Grace and Free Will*, Bk. I, 17 (PL 44, 901).

[41]*The Grace of Christ and Original Sin*, Chap. 37, 42 (CSEL 42, 200).

[42]*Against Julian*, Bk. 5, Chap. 11 (PL 44, 809).

[43]*Summa Theologiae*, I, q. 49, a. 1, ad 3. See also q. 48, a. 5 and *De malo*, q. 2, a. 2 (Parma: Peter Fiaccador, Tome VIII [1856], p. 238).

[44]*Summa Theologiae*, I, q. 48, a. 2.

[45]I, q. 48, a. 2, ad 3.

[46]*Summa Theologiae*, I-II, q. 82, a. 3.

[47]I-II, q. 82, a. 1.

[48]I-II, q. 82, a. 1, ad 2.

[49]I-II, q. 81, a. 1.

[50]I-II, q. 83, a. 1.

[51]I-II, q. 83, a. 3 and a. 4.

[52]*De malo*, q. 5, a. 3 (Parma: pp. 302-303).

[53]See G. W. F. Hegel, *Phenomenology of Spirit*. Transl. by A. V. Miller with analysis of the text and foreword by J. N. Findlay (Oxford: Clarendon Press, 1977), nos. 17-18.

[54]*Ibid.*, no. 20.

[55]Cf. *ibid.*, nos. 25 and 596.

[56]*Ibid.*, no. 468.

[57]*Ibid.*, no. 775.

[58]*Ibid.*, no. 178.

[59]*Ibid.*, nos. 178-196.

[60]Cf. *ibid.*, nos. 672-683.

[61]*Writings in Time of War* (New York: Harper & Row, 1968), p. 98.

[62]Cf. *Writings in Time of War*, pp. 164 and 172.

[63]*Ibid.*, p. 103.

[64]See "Reflections on Original Sin," *Christianity and Evolution* (New York: Harcourt Brace Jovanovich, Inc., 1971), pp. 191-196.

[65]"The Spirit of Earth," *Building the Earth* (New York: Avon Books, 1965), pp. 64-65.

[66]*Systematic Theology*, Vol. II (Chicago: The University of Chicago Press, 1957), pp. 19-28.

[67]*Systematic Theology*, Vol. II, p. 29.

[68]*Systematic Theology*, Vol. I (Chicago: The University of Chicago Press, 1951), p. 202.

[69]*Systematic Theology,* Vol. II, p. 44.

[70]*Systematic Theology,* Vol. II, p. 38.

[71]*Ibid.,* p. 40, cf. p. 56.

[72]*Systematic Theology,* Vol. II, p. 43.

[73]*Systematic Theology,* Vol. II, p. 75.

[74]So comments Walter Lowe, *Mystery and the Unconscious: A Study in the Thought of Paul Ricoeur* (Metuchen, N.J.: Scarecrow, 1977), p. 12.

[75]"(a) the subject's *opening* to the world or field or objects, (b) the *here* or concrete position from which the field is perceived, and (c) the originating *motion* which allows objects to appear from different sides and which points to the body as the condition for perspective"; so explains Don Ihde, *Hermeneutic Phenomenology: The Philosophy of Paul Ricoeur* (Evanston, Ill.: Northwestern University Press, 1971), p. 67.

[76]Patrick Bourgeois, *Extension of Ricoeur's Hermeneutic* (The Hague: Martinus Nijhoff, 1975), p. 44.

[77]Cited by Bourgeois, p. 39.

[78]*The Symbolism of Evil* (Boston: Beacon Press, 1969), p. 254. See *L'Homme faillible* (p. 147) as cited by Bourgeois on pp. 55-56: "Only a being who wants the all and who schematizes it in the objects of human desire is able to make a mistake, that is, take his object for the *absolute, forget* the symbolic character of the bond between happiness and an object of desire; this forgetting makes the symbol an idol; the impassioned life becomes a passional existence. This forgetting, this birth of the idol, of servitude and passional sufferance, leads to a hermeneutics of the passions which we will undertake elsewhere. But it was necessary to show the point of impact of the passions in a primordial affection which is the very locus of fallibility. The restless devotedness of the impassioned is like the primordial innocence of the passional, and at the same time the essential fragility from where it originated. Nowhere better than in the relation of the impassioned to the passional do we understand that the structures of fallibility make up the pre-existing ground of fault." A similar thought occurs in Ricoeur's article "The Problem of the Will and Philosophical Discourse." "The will," he says, "appears then as an interior dialectic between an infinite exegence which reflects its limitless power of self-assertion and the task of self-realization in a finite reality. Individuality is nothing else than this confrontation between the endlessness of reflection and the finitude of actualization." See *Patterns of the Life-World,* eds. James M. Edie, Francis H. Parker and Calvin O. Schrag (Evanston: Northwestern University Press, 1970), p. 282.

[79]See *Freedom and Nature: The Voluntary and the Involuntary* (Evanston, Ill.: Northwestern University Press, 1966), p. 29.

[80]*Ibid.,* p. 100; cf. p. 98.

[81]*Ibid.,* p. 61.

[82]*Ibid.,* p. 62.

[83]*Ibid.,* p. 196.

[84]*Ibid.,* p. 477.

[85]*Fallible Man* (Chicago: Henry Regnery, 1965), p. 224.

[86]See the position of A. Hulsbosch, *God's Creation* (London: Sheed and Ward, 1965), pp. 40-41, 50.

[87]Erich Fromm, *The Anatomy of Human Destructiveness* (New York: Holt, Rinehart and Winston, 1973), p. 2.

[88]This is the kind of explanation that is marked as inadequate in "The Hartford Declaration" (1975): "Theme 7: *Since what is human is good, evil can adequately be understood as failure to realize human potential.* This theme invites false under-

standing of the ambivalence of human existence and underestimates the pervasiveness of sin. Paradoxically, by minimizing the enormity of evil, it undermines serious and sustained attacks on particular social or individual evils." *Theology Today,* 32 (1976), p. 96.

[89]Z. Alszeghy, S.J., and M. Flick, S.J., "Il peccato originale in prospettiva personalistica," *Gregorianum,* 46 (1965), pp. 705-732. Also, "Il peccato originale in prospettiva evoluzionistica," *Gregorianum,* 47 (1966), pp. 201-225.

[90]See also *A New Catechism* (New York: Herder and Herder, 1967), p. 264: "In a world of ascending evolution, sin is often nothing but the refusal to grow in the direction which conscience reveals."

[91]*Evolution and Guilt* (Maryknoll, N.Y.: Orbis Books, 1974), p. 23.

[92]See p. 38.

[93]See p. 58.

[94]p. 108.

[95]See p. 127.

[96]Cf. P. Smulders, *The Design of Teilhard de Chardin* (Westminster, Md.: The Newman Press, 1966), Chapters 6 and 7.

[97]See John Hick, *Evil and the God of Love* (New York: Harper & Row, 1966), p. 220.

[98]*A Theology for the Social Gospel,* p. 67, cited in Reinhold Niebuhr, *The Nature and Destiny of Man* (New York: C. Scribner's Sons, 1941), p. 246.

[99]*Man and Sin* (Notre Dame, Ind.: University of Notre Dame Press, 1965).

[100]*Vatican Council II: The Conciliar and Post Conciliar Documents,* ed. A. Flannery, O.P. (Collegeville, Minn.: The Liturgical Press, 1975), Art. 25, p. 926.

[101]Cf. Vatican Council II's "Dogmatic Constitution on the Church," Art. 15-16, pp. 366-368.

[102]"The Dogmatic Constitution on the Church," Art. 8, p. 358.

[103]E. Fromm, *The Forgotten Language: An Introduction to the Understanding of Dreams, Fairy Tales, and Myths* (New York: Rinehart, 1951), pp. 47-48.

[104]See E. Fromm, *The Forgotten Language,* pp. 53-54.

[105]*Freud and Original Sin* (Paramus, N.J.: Paulist Press, 1974), p. 105.

[106]See p. 107. Note also p. 85: "A man is what he loves; this is the essence of psycho-analytic theory."

[107]Cf. Reinhold Niebuhr: "In Marxist thought the emergence of private property represents a kind of 'Fall' in the history of mankind." *The Children of Light and the Children of Darkness* (New York: C. Scribner's Sons, 1944), p. 90.

[108]See C. K. Barrett, *A Commentary on the Epistle to the Romans* (New York: Harper & Row, 1957), pp. 138-153. Cf. Jer 31:31-34; Ezek 36:24-27.

[109]*The Idea of Freedom,* Vol. 1 (New York: Doubleday, 1958), p. 614.

[110]*Reaping the Whirlwind: A Christian Interpretation of History* (New York: The Seabury Press, 1976), p. 124.

[111]*The Nature and Destiny of Man: A Christian Interpretation.* 1. *Human Nature* (New York: C. Scribner's Sons, 1949), p. 178. Note Niebuhr's later misgivings about using the theological symbol of original sin—notwithstanding its correctness—to confront and to challenge modern optimism: *Man's Nature and His Communities* (New York: C. Scribner's Sons, 1965), pp. 23-24.

[112]R. Niebuhr, *The Nature and Destiny of Man,* p. 181.

[113]*Freedom and Nature: The Voluntary and the Involuntary,* p. 98.

[114]*Ibid.,* p. 103.

[115]*Walden Two* (New York: The MacMillan Co., 1948; paperback 1962), p. 104.

[116]*Freedom and Nature,* p. 6.

[117]*Ibid.,* p. 84. See also this later statement of Ricoeur: ". . . man may *designate*

his actions as his intentions, *justify* them by the reasons for which he claims to perform them, and *ascribe them to himself as the agent of his own doing."* *Political and Social Essays,* collected and edited by D. Stewart and J. Bien (Athens: Ohio University Press, 1974), p. 57.

[118]The will is defined by V. Bourke as follows: "Willing is that psychic activity of man, whereby he tends toward or away from certain objectives reflectively adopted, whereby he sometimes achieves personal freedom of action, whereby he acts with some spontaneity or self-initiative, and whereby he approves or loves what he deems good and disapproves or hates what he deems not good." *Will in Western Thought: An Historical Survey* (New York: Sheed and Ward, 1964), p. 235.

[119]Book X, 617. See *The Republic of Plato,* translated with introduction and notes by Francis M. Cornford (New York: Oxford University Press, 1945), p. 355.

[120]*On Grace and Free Will,* Chap. 15 (PL 44, 899).

[121]*Freedom and Nature,* p. 342.

[122]P. Ricoeur, *Ibid.,* p. 164.

[123]*Political and Social Essays,* p. 35.

Chapter 2

Disunity: The Symbol of Sin

In the previous chapter we examined the basic conditions of the possibility of moral failure. In this chapter we will examine the symbol of disunity as a central expression of the condition of human failure.

Disunity as a linguistic symbol points to a malaise in the midst of human life, a malaise that precedes one's reflection and choice. It points to structures that lead to moral failure. It points to an evil heart that itself is the source of evil action. It refers to a basic fault that goes back in time to the origin of the human species and that abides throughout the centuries. It points to a faulty relationship between God and his human creation. The symbol of disunity is a figure of the broken covenant that was established by God and was meant to endure throughout the ages of humankind. In short, disunity is a perceptible and referential symbol. It brings the Christian mind to focus on an important, if terrifying, dimension of human existence in this universe.

1. Symbol

Broadly speaking, a symbol is a perceptible reality that represents or points to some other reality. In one sense the symbol is like a sign for a sign too points to some other reality. For our purposes, however, we may regard the sign as a more literal or direct indication of another reality, e.g., a road sign indicates quite directly a speed limit or a no parking zone. The symbol has a richer consistency, both as a perceptible object and as a reality signified. The symbol brings together the perceived object and the signified reality. This is a general description of symbol. There are, of course, many definitions of symbol which vary from field to field and from thinker to thinker. Here by way of illustration we may sketch the ways in which Paul Tillich and Paul Ricoeur define the concept of symbol.

The concept of symbol bulks large in the philosophical and theological thinking of Paul Tillich. Over a period of five decades he works with the notion of symbol and returns to it frequently in his writings. He sums up his thought in an article which was published four years before his death: "The Meaning and Justification of Religious Symbols."[1]

The symbol, as he elaborates the term, should be called representative. He distinguishes the representative symbol from mere signs such as mathematical and logical symbols or road signs. Tillich lists five characteristics of the representative symbol.

1) The symbol points beyond itself. It must indeed be perceived concretely or imaginatively, but it points beyond itself to another reality. The perceptible symbol may be "the ordinary meaning of a word, the empirical reality of a historical figure, the traits of a human face (in a painting), a human catastrophe (in a drama), a human power or virtue (in a description of the divine)."[2] The perceptible symbol points to and expresses a reality that cannot be grasped directly and that must be expressed through the symbol.

2) The representative symbol participates in the reality that it refers to and expresses. The symbol both represents and draws power from the symbolized reality. An emissary, for instance, represents an institution and participates in the honor that he or she receives.

3) While signs are created and dismissed according to convenience, the symbol cannot be created at will. Individuals may indeed assist the birth of a symbol, but it becomes a representative symbol only through the reactive acceptance of a group. Conversely, it dies when the group ceases to recognize it or to accept it.

4) The representative symbol opens up dimensions of reality that are otherwise closed to the human spirit. "Religious symbols mediate ultimate reality through things, persons, events which because of their mediating functions receive the quality of 'holy.' In the experience of holy places, times, books, words, images, and acts, symbols of the holy reveal something of the 'Holy-Itself' and produce the experience of holiness in persons and groups."[3]

5) The symbol has the power of integration and disintegration. The representative symbol integrates when it elevates, quiets, stabilizes, and heals individuals or groups. The symbol causes disintegration when it produces restlessness, depression, anxiety, fanaticism. Examples of integrating symbols: "a king, an event, a document in the political realm of representative symbolism, an epic work, architectural symbols, a holy figure, a holy book, a holy rite in religion." Examples of disintegrating symbols: "some political symbols such as the Führer and the swastika, . . . religious symbols such as the Moloch type of gods, human sacrifices, doctrinal symbols producing a split consciousness."[4]

Briefly, the religious symbol is "material taken out of the world of finite things, to point beyond itself to the ground of being and meaning, to being itself and meaning itself. As a symbol it participates in the power of the ultimate to which it points; or, to use a word which we commonly use when we speak of the power of ultimate being, it participates in the 'holy.'"[5]

William Rowe succinctly summarizes Tillich's thought on symbol: "Thus in addition to the basic claim that symbols participate in the reality of that to which they point, Tillich claims that symbols (1) open up levels of reality which are otherwise closed to us, (2) unlock dimensions and elements of our soul which correspond to the dimensions and elements of reality, (3) cannot be produced or replaced intentionally and (4) grow and die."[6] It is particularly significant that symbols are revelatory. They disclose and refer to levels of reality that lie beyond the symbols themselves. They not only provide insight into another reality, but they also participate in that reality.

It is also significant that revelatory symbols are analogous. There is a real comparison between the finite reality that becomes a symbol and the reality symbolized. The analogous character of the symbol insures its revelatory dimension; the symbol expresses in a correlative way the reality to which it points.

For our purposes it is important to note that words, too, can be symbols. The word "church" points to a religious assembly. The word "Messiah" points to a kingly, servant, and exalted reality in Jesus.[7] Liturgical formulas, too, are symbols, referring as they do to a divine and transcendent reality. Myths are more elaborate symbols; they are "symbols of faith combined in stories about divine-human encounters."[8]

Both Ricoeur and Tillich acknowledge linguistic dimensions of the symbol. For Ricoeur in particular the symbol must be brought to verbal expression in order to function as an authentic symbol. Ricoeur disagrees with those who hold that symbols have nothing to do with language.[9] For both Ricoeur and Tillich a word or a phrase may itself be a symbol, a perceptible reality that points to another reality. It is especially the symbolic value of words that is of importance in this study, for we have selected the words "disunity" and "community" as highly charged with meaning. They are capable of containing and referring to multiple levels of the human experience of sin and grace.

Paul Ricoeur analyzes and uses the structure of symbol in his phenomenology and hermeneutics. The symbol is a major concept in *The Symbolism of Evil,*[10] a part of his general study of the philosophy of will. For Ricoeur, the symbol is a sign, to be sure, but it is also more than a sign. A sign may be arbitrary (a red light means stop), but a symbol is never entirely arbitrary; there is always some natural relationship between the symbol and its significance.

What is the sequence of the development of the symbol? First there is the experience, then the expression in symbolic form, and finally there is the interpretation of the symbol. The symbol is an expression that communicates a meaning. In fact, it has a double significance: it has a literal meaning and a figurative meaning. The symbol means something in itself and at the same time it intends something else. Ricoeur says, "Thus a symbol is a double-meaning linguistic expression that requires an interpretation, and interpretation is a work of understanding that aims at deciphering symbols."[11] A perception of the primary meaning of the symbol leads to a knowledge of its latent meaning.

The three dimensions, functions, or modalities of every authentic symbol are cosmic, oneiric, and poetic. The cosmic dimension deals with the symbol as a reality of the cosmos, e.g., the sun, the moon, the waters, the vegetation. The oneiric dimension deals with the dream modality of the symbol; Ricoeur refers particularly to the way in which dreams symbolize the unconscious strivings of the human psyche. The poetic modality brings the symbol to verbal expression.[12] Ricoeur's theme throughout *The Symbolism of Evil* is that the symbol itself gives rise to thought.[13] An encounter with the symbol provokes thought and verbal expression.[14]

Myths are species of symbols, "developed in the form of narrations and articulated in a time and a space that cannot be co-ordinated with the time and space of history and geography according to the critical method."[15] Myths, therefore, are secondary in comparison with such primary symbols as deviation, captivity, stain, guilt, and sin.[16]

In a later work, *The Conflict of Interpretations,* Ricoeur elaborates and develops his notion of symbol as he pursues the subject of interpretation. "I define 'symbol'," he says, "as any structure of signification in which a direct, primary, literal meaning designates, in addition, another meaning which is indirect, secondary, and figurative and which can be apprehended only through the first."[17] The symbol is a reality of the world of experience, something that can be perceived directly and immediately. "Whether we are dealing with the stain image in the magical conception of evil as pollution, or with deviation images of the crooked path, of transgression, of wandering or error, in the more ethical conception of sin, or with the weight image of a burden in the more interiorized experience of guilt—in all these cases the symbol of evil is constituted by starting from something which has a first-level meaning and is borrowed from the experience of nature—of contact, of man's orientation in space."[18] The symbol is taken from the world of human experience, but it points beyond the immediate experience and beyond itself to another meaning. The literal symbol is the path to revelation, to the opening up of a reality in the world of human existence.

In his later writings the symbol continues to hold an important place in Ricoeur's thought on interpretation. He acknowledges that hermeneutics is broader than an interpretation of the double meaning of the symbol, but the symbol is still the prime example of hermeneutics. Ricoeur says:

> I readily grant today that the interpretation of symbols is not the whole of hermeneutics, but I continue to hold that it is the condensation point and, if I may say so, the place of greatest density, because it is in the symbol that language is revealed in its strongest force and with its greatest fullness. It says something independently of me, and it says more than I can understand. The symbol is surely the privileged place of the experience of the surplus of meaning.[19]

Words, too, are symbols, or as Ricoeur says, "Words are signs in speech position."[20] The word "father," for instance, can function as a symbol, specifically as a symbol of God: "As a symbol it [father] would be a parable of the ground of love; it would be the counterpart, in a theology of love, of the progression which led us from a mere resignation to Fate to a poetic life."[21] Words assume meaning in the context of a sentence. They have a richness which can give them multiple meanings, though they can also be directed univocally to one significance. If the words are used with a richness of meanings, they function as multidimensional symbols:

> If the context tolerates or even preserves several isotopies at the same time, we will be dealing with an actually symbolic language, which, in saying *one* thing, says something else. Instead of sifting out one dimension of meaning, the context allows several to pass, indeed consolidates several of them, which run together in the manner of the superimposed texts of a palimpsest. The polysemy of our words is then liberated. Thus the poem allows all the semantic values to be mutually reinforced.[22]

Ricoeur comes to the view that symbols have a semantic and non-semantic character: "Within the symbol, it now seems to me, there is something nonsemantic as well as something semantic . . . ."[23] Ricoeur's thought confirms our search for verbal symbols of the condition of sin.

2. Original Sin as a Symbol

What was the import of the symbol of original sin? What was the reality to which the symbol referred? It will be necessary here to sketch out the significance of this symbol in order to understand its translation and development into the symbol of disunity. To be sure, the meaning of the symbol of original sin changed frequently in the course of history, but the broad features of the symbol were rather standard as the theology of original sin was developed through the centuries.

The term "original sin" does not occur in the Bible nor in the early creeds of the Church. This is not to say, however, that much of the reality expressed by the term is not found in Scripture or supposed in the creeds. The term articulated a doctrine of sin that was disclosed in the community of Israel, in the person of Jesus, and in the writings of the New Testament. It was felt that a non-biblical term was appropriate or even necessary to express and to defend a significant Christian doctrine. We may recall two related cases in the history of doctrine: the use of the term *homoousios* in the Council of Nicea (325) to defend the divine Lordship of the Son, and the use of the term *transsubstantiatio* in the Council of Trent (1545-63) to defend the reality of the presence of Christ in the eucharistic meal. The term "original sin" functioned in a similar way, though there is some question about whether it received a strict definition in the Council of Trent.

It is not clear who precisely introduced the Latin term *peccatum originale* (original sin). It was in use before Augustine's major works on the subject,[24] though it was Augustine who pondered deeply on the topic of original sin and whose teaching directed theology and catechesis up to very recent times. Augustine, assuredly, did not invent the reality of original sin, contrary to the accusation of Julian of Eclanum.[25] He used the term to summarize a reality which was already in the minds of Christian believers.

The term *peccatum originale* has been part of Christian theology and catechesis for over fifteen hundred years, at least in the West. The word *peccatum* (sin) indicates that the verbal symbol expresses a situation that can be called sin. The word "sin" in the term "original sin," however, is understood analogously to the notion of personal, voluntary sin. The proper notion of sin is the willful, deliberate, moral failure of a person. Any other reality that is called sin can only be understood in reference to personal sin. Original sin, therefore, has meaning only in reference to voluntary, personal sin. The word "sin" in the symbol "original sin" has the advantage of pointing to the seriousness of the situation. The reality expressed by the symbol is so destructive of the relationship humans have to each other and to God that it can be expressed by the word "sin."

The second word of the symbol, *originale* (original), points to the origin of the sinful condition. The origin was understood in a twofold fashion: 1) the historical origin of the sin at the beginning of human history; 2) the underlying sin that is already present when any person begins human life. Scholastic theologians called the first situation *peccatum originale originans* (the sin in the beginning that initiates the condition of sin) and the second situation *peccatum originale originatum* (the condition of sin as it touches a person coming into existence after the historical beginning of sin). In general, the term original sin depicted the sin of Adam in the beginning and the whole "sinful" condition that resulted from the beginning of sin: a moral, spiritual, and physical disaster affecting the life of every human being. It was a short expression, almost a theological code word, that summed up an immense amount of teaching about the existence of sin in the world: separation from God, the wrath of God, condemnation, ignorance, suffering, death. It was a brief way of expressing the negative side of redemption in Christ. Original sin expressed the situation from which Christ in principle redeemed the whole of humankind.

It was always difficult to explain how the sin of an ancient ancestor could cause the guilt of someone born at a great remove in time and history. It never seemed quite fair to burden someone born later with the guilt of someone who lived and sinned in the beginning of human history. Theologians submitted various attempts to explain later inclusion in the guilt of Adam. Some examples: the whole of humankind was seen as one giant body moved by the will of Adam; or Adam was viewed as the juridical head of the human race and his decision counted for all; or one invoked the concept of corporate personality according to which one person could represent a whole group of persons; or one said that God decided to transmit the grace of friendship on condition that the first man passed the test of obedience. These and other theological explanations dulled the sharp edges of the traditional teaching, but they did not prove wholly satisfying. The gnawing question remained: why should an individual receive a deprived and depraved nature when he or she was not personally responsible for the original offense against God?

Since the earliest centuries of the Church, the baptism of infants was viewed as the test case of original sin. Baptism was conferred unto the remission of sins, that is, in view of the presence of sin. The New Testament contains no clear evidence that infants were baptized, but the practice of infant baptism began within a century of the New Testament period. It was clear to everyone, of course, that infants could not commit personal sins. Baptism unto the remission of sins, therefore, could only mean that they incurred guilt by reason of their birth in this world, by reason of their descent from Adam. They shared Adam's guilt because they stemmed from him by way of physical generation. Augustine insisted that, if infants were not sinners, they would not be baptized and would not be related to Christ who came to call sinners and to die for them.

Adults were baptized unto the remission of sins, both the forgiveness of their personal sins and the remission of the sin which they contracted from Adam by way of human generation.

The most authoritative and official statement of the church on original sin occurred in the Council of Trent, the Roman Catholic Church's belated response to the Protestant reformers and to its own movement of reform from within. While the council began its deliberations in December of 1545 and held its final session in December of 1563, it was actually in progress and enacted decrees only during three periods (1545-1547/ 49; 1551-1552; 1562-1563). The decree on original sin was promulgated during the first period, on June 17, 1546. The decree was prepared in less than four weeks (May 24 to June 17), a length of time that was hardly sufficient to propose and to debate a complete doctrine of original sin.

However, the matter of original sin must have been deemed important in the Protestant-Catholic controversy, for the discussion of the issue was put on the agenda early in the council, right after the publication of a decree on sacred Scripture and traditions (April 8, 1546) and immediately before a discussion of justification.

The point of controversy between the Protestants and the Catholics was not the existence of original sin. The presence of original sin was an accepted and traditional teaching of all the controversialists. The points at issue were the nature of original sin, the effects of original sin after baptism, and the efficacy of the baptism of infants. The controversy between the Catholics and Martin Luther focused on the nature of original sin, more specifically on the effects of original sin after baptism. The controversy between the Catholics and the Anabaptists concerned the practice of infant baptism.

Martin Luther used chiefly biblical and Augustinian terms to define hereditary or original sin (*Erbsünde*): evil inclination, concupiscence, lack of trust in God, lack of fear of God, etc. For Luther concupiscence is an apt description of the state of original sin, for concupiscence characterizes human opposition to God and inclination toward evil. Even the baptized person experiences the opposition and inclination, but because of his or her baptism the guilt (*reatus*) of the sin is remitted. Sinful inclinations and sin itself remain, but they are not imputed in view of the merits of Jesus Christ. "The sin that is left in his flesh is not imputed to him. This is because Christ, who is entirely without sin, has now become one with his Christian and intercedes for him with the Father."[26] Luther calls the evil inclination that remains after baptism *sin*. This leaves the impression that the root of original sin is not removed in baptism. The Council of Trent insists on its removal. But in point of fact, Luther does not deny that the baptized person becomes justified, holy, and gifted by the Holy Spirit. He says:

> The words GRACE and GIFT differ inasmuch as the true meaning of grace is the kindness or favour which God bears towards us of His own choice, and through which He is willing to give us Christ, and to pour the Holy Spirit and His blessings upon us. Paul makes this clear in chapter 5 [Rom 5:15f.] when he speaks of the grace and favour of Christ, and the like. Nevertheless, both the gifts and the spirit must be received by us daily; although even then they will be incomplete; for the old desires and sins still linger in us, and strive against the spirit. . . .[27]

Luther's primary concern is that humans cannot make a move toward God on their own power. It is God who provides forgiveness and justification in Jesus Christ.

The theologians and fathers of the Council of Trent did not understand their task as the promulgation of a new interpretation of the doctrine of original sin. They were generally steeped in the tradition of the

Church and desired to cite the tradition as a way of opposing the teachings of the Protestant reformers. In a few matters they extended or clarified the traditional teaching as a way of opposing directly specific positions of the Lutherans or Anabaptists. Some few participants in the council, it is true, proposed minor theological elaborations of the traditional doctrine.

Trent's first two canons explicitly repeat the teaching of Canons 1 and 2 of the II Council of Orange (529), a provincial council gathered under the leadership of Saint Caesarius of Arles.[28] Its decrees were signed by 14 bishops and 8 laymen. While the decrees of Orange were not those of a general council, and while they only gradually became known in the course of the middle ages, they were particularly significant because they crystalized the teaching of Saint Augustine and were approved by Pope Boniface II in 531.[29]

The repetition of Orange makes evident the desire to tie the decree of Trent to the traditional teaching of the Church, especially to the teaching that was elaborated in the Pelagian-Augustinian controversy. Some late medieval theologians may very well have been semi-Pelagian in thought;[30] but the theologians and fathers of Trent wished to make their anti-Pelagian doctrine very clear, especially since the Protestant reformers perceived Catholic thought, or at least Catholic practice, as Pelagian.

Neither Catholics nor Protestants denied the historicity of Adam, his blessed life in paradise, his fall, his loss of divine friendship, his subsequent sufferings and death. The point of controversy did not turn on the historicity of Adam. Thus the council did not strictly define anything on the subject of his historical person and fall. It assumed his life in paradise, his loss of the paradisiacal gifts through sin, his loss of holiness and justice (the scholastic way of defining the core of original sin), and his subjection to the wrath of God, to death, and to slavery to Satan (the biblical/Augustinian way of defining the condition of sin).[31] The council insisted on the traditional doctrine that Adam transmitted to his posterity a death which is a real sin.[32]

The council repeated the anti-Pelagian doctrine that Adam's sin (one in origin) is transmitted by way of propagation, not by imitation. The council refrained from indicating the manner of propagation. It repeated the traditional teaching that Adam's sin is transmitted to everyone and that it exists in each person as his or her own. It repeated the anti-Pelagian teaching that the merits of Jesus Christ, not the forces of human nature, take away the sin. It defended the traditional practice of infant baptism.[33]

In particular the council wanted to declare that the whole character of sin, the guilt (*reatus*) of original sin, is removed through the grace of Christ and the sacrament of baptism. It characterized the concupiscence that remains after baptism, not as real sin, but only as a result of sin, a trial, and an incitement to sin.[34] This statement on concupiscence was particularly important because it was directed against the Lutheran (or what was believed to be the Lutheran position, though it is not mentioned specifically) that concupiscence as sin remains after baptism.

What is the thrust of the council's decree on original sin? What is the import of the decree? Vanneste and Schmied hold that the Council of Trent did not define the nature of original sin.[35] Gutwenger holds that there is nothing irreformable in the teachings of Trent on original sin, that it is safe teaching without being dogmatic.[36] Alszeghy and Flick, however, find something that is dogmatically decreed in the Council of Trent, but even they are very cautious in their statement: "What is said about the grace of Christ communicated in baptism is taught so proximately that it is virtually beyond historical contingency or the possibility of reformulation. What is said about sin and its transmission and about concupiscence is asserted only indirectly and in function of an existing historical situation."[37] The grace of Christ that remits sin is indeed the center of the decree of Trent, but we hold that it is not beyond reformulation. Every statement, dogmatic or otherwise, is formulated according to the mentality and verbal expression of a particular time and as such is capable of interpretation and reformulation. The basic thrust of the dogmatic statement, however, abides into the future. In this case, the basic thrust of the decree is the reference to the grace of Christ that is transmitted through baptism. It seems, moreover, that the council made some direct statements about sin and its transmission and about concupiscence (contrary to Alszeghy-Flick's conclusion). These direct statements about sin, however, are made in the context of the historical situation (the Catholic-Protestant controversy) and in function of the primary concern of the decree (Christ's grace).

It seems clear from this survey of the decree that the theologians and fathers of Trent do not propose a complete exposition of the doctrine of original sin. They repeat many features of the traditional teaching, features that are not called into question in the 16th century. They also refine or express differently other features of the traditional teaching to meet the needs of the 16th century Church, specifically to oppose aspects of Protestant theologies of original sin.

The council assumes, and therefore does not define, these traditional dimensions of original sin: the historicity of Adam; the unicity of Adam; the existence of a paradise in the beginning; the sin of Adam in paradise; Adam's loss of holiness and justice; his subjection to ignorance, suffering, and death; his spiritual death; the transmission of guilt (*reatus*) to Adam's posterity; the loss of holiness and justice and the presence of sin and death in his posterity. These aspects of the teaching are assumed generally by all the controversialists and are not in question.

There are other aspects of the doctrine of original sin which the council insists on, refines, and promulgates to meet the crisis of the 16th century: the inability of a person to justify himself or herself (against real and assumed Pelagian thinking of the time); the "dead" condition of a person in sin; the existence of original sin (without a specific definition); the forgiveness of sin in the merits of Jesus Christ; the efficacy of infant baptism; the removal of sin in baptism; the declaration that the inclination to sin (concupiscence) is not itself sin.

These lists are not exhaustive but they contain most of the concerns of the participants in Trent. The theologians and fathers of Trent proclaim loudly the existence of sin, the incapacity of a person to extricate himself or herself from the death of sin, the value of baptism, both for infants and for adults, and the presence of non-sinful temptations to sin.

3. Disunity as a Multivalent and Integrating Symbol

A symbol is not confined to one point of reference. It is heavy with meanings and points to multiple levels of signification. It may be that one meaning is central in relation to others, but the points of reference are many.

The symbol of disunity is multivalent. It points to many divisions that exist in the world of Christian and human experience. The primary division is one that exists between God and humans. The symbol of disunity supposes a certain ontological distance between God and humankind, but this distance is not the main thrust of the symbol. The symbol of disunity points to an unfortunate division between God and human beings, a kind of division that ought not to exist, a division that is created by moral failure on the part of humans. It is not God who withdraws from the relationship or who wishes to reduce the relationship to one of non-involved metaphysical distance. His relationship to the human community remains steady and close. Human persons, however, by benign neglect of God, by actual hatred of his position in the universe, by refusing to follow his lead to the level of maximum communion in the universe, are able to, and do in fact break the unity linking God and themselves.

The symbol of disunity points to another basic division in the world. It is the division that exists between one nation and another, one society and another, one culture and another. The symbol is not concerned directly with the divisions that are unavoidable in the development of peoples around the world. The various peoples and societies unfold their potentialities differently and thereby create divisions which are really in the realm of beautiful variety. But nations also develop in competition with others, in active conflict with others, in hostile opposition to others. One nation actively oppresses another, curtails its development. It does this for national gain and esteem. This is a moral issue. Here natural division is turned into disunity, a separation between peoples that results from moral failure on the part of national leaders and of many others.

There are natural divisions in families and other small groups. Here again the divisions are exacerbated by lack of cooperation, by self-will, by hatred. The natural distance in families and groups becomes sinful disunity through moral failure on the part of members of the families and groups.

Finally, there is an inevitable distance between one person and another. One person cannot be united with another to the point of absorption. Persons remain unique and individual in their relationship to other persons. But the natural division is increased by self-love and hatred. One person creates disunity by isolating self from others, by seeking self to the point of damaging others. A morally sinful relationship between persons increases and flourishes.

The symbol for the willfully and morally deficient relationships that exist in our universe is disunity. The symbol of disunity points to the lack of unity that exists as a result of moral failure, the lack of unity that exists on all levels of personal relationships: God, nation, society, family, group, Church. The one symbol of disunity is multivalent. It points to the many levels of morally responsible divisions that exist in our world.

A valid symbol is one that can integrate within itself a multiplicity of meanings. The integrating character of the symbol is surely related to its multivalent dimension. In each case there is consideration of one symbol which points to a variety of meanings. The multivalent dimension of the symbol, however, stresses the multiplicity of the realities symbolized or signified, while the integrating character of the symbol stresses the literal symbol itself and its capacity to draw together a broad range of signified realities.

The symbol of disunity is such that it can bring to focus a multiplicity of realities in our universe. The one symbol indicates the whole range of dividedness, from a hateful distance between God and humans to the unloving distance between one human being and another. It concentrates in a word the fostered misunderstandings between peoples and the contrived ambiguities of daily language. It manifests the lack of integrity in human verbal exchange, from insincere promises to colored narrations, from selective recollections to vain purposes.

The symbol of disunity allows access to a concentrated grasp of the divisive elements in the human situation. The one symbol allows a glimpse of the magnitude of division that exists in the universe, that is present at every level of experience, that touches all aspects of human life. The symbol of disunity sums up the whole extent of dividedness and brings it into sharp focus. In this way the whole weight of disunity bears down upon the person who observes the symbol and who realizes its ramifications.

No symbol exhaustively expresses the reality to which it points. The symbol is only more or less effective in indicating the signified reality. This is true because there is no absolute identity between the symbol and the point of reference; if there were absolute identity, there would be no need for the symbol, or rather, the symbol itself would be the reality.

Disunity as a symbol expresses in great measure the reality of sin, but not in an exhaustive manner. The symbol of disunity is only more or less effective in containing and expressing the condition of moral failure that results in dividedness between God and humans, between nation and nation, and between one person and another.

There is an analogical relationship between the symbol of disunity and the reality contained in the symbol. A grasp of the symbol leads to an understanding of the content of moral failure, and vice versa, a grasp of the human condition assists the understanding of the symbol of disunity which expresses the condition. Analogy, of course, is not a one-to-one relationship. There are lines of reference between the analogues. So too with the symbol of disunity and the content of the symbol. There are connecting lines between the symbol and the reality symbolized. For instance, the symbol of disunity expresses a failure, some wrong-doing on the part of someone; it expresses the alienation from God, others, and self that arises from moral deviation.

Analogy, therefore, is two-way. The reality of sin is allowed perceptual and conceptual grasp by means of the symbol of disunity. The symbol portrays analogically the reality which lies deep within the human heart, the human community, the human world, and the divine-human sphere. The symbol as an expression is never completely adequate; but if it is valid at all, it manifests and brings to light some lines of comparison between the human condition and the symbol itself. The symbol of disunity leads the mind analogically to the deep rift that is experienced in the midst of human life.

4. Disunity and Freedom of the Will

The symbol of disunity indicates that human freedom is involved in the sinful condition of humankind. Freedom is able to fail the individual, the human community, the universe, and God. Human freedom is able to put distance between self and the other person by decisions which disregard the value and excellence of the other. It is a freedom that has gone astray, pursuing goals and conveniences contrary to the real good of the other. Without freedom there can be failures of various kinds, but not moral failures. Moral failures or sins assume and require the dimension of freedom. Why freedom fails is beyond ultimate explanation and clarification. The will is certainly set upon by many factors, both interior to the self and exterior, but ultimately the will is free to choose the failure.

If there were no freedom, there would be no reason to talk of moral evil or moral failure; a doctrine of determinism would suffice. But freedom of the will is assumed here, and thus it must be stated that the symbol of disunity points to a volitional aspect of human action: moral failure that is freely accepted.

A self-centered will lacks a basic unity in its inner life and dynamism. Disunity is the ultimate characteristic of the will that is not master in its own house and that shuts itself off from others. The will finds itself disintegrated and scattered. Its various energies and drives bear it off in different directions. It is pulled in the direction of self-love and narcissistic adulation; at the same time it feels the call to achievements for the sake of others. It feels the need to act vigorously in order to achieve a place in the sun, in order to acquire the very needs of human existence; yet it must continually compete with others who seek a place in the same sun and who are required to work to gain the needs of existence. The will feels the need to seek private gain, to hold on to possessions, to retain them even in the face of community needs. The will views itself as the center of all needs and attentions; yet it looks out on a world in which it is just one unit. It regards the whole universe as a reality at its disposal; yet it must share the universe with others.

Vatican Council II's "The Church in the Modern World" notes the disunity in the individual and in society: "Man therefore is divided in himself. As a result, the whole life of men, both individual and social, shows itself to be a struggle, and a dramatic one, between good and evil, between light and darkness."[38] There is a basic discontinuity and disunity between the individual and the community (family, state, world). The needs of the individual and those of the community are never in perfect harmony, since there is always tug and pull in the relationship. There are times when the individual demands too much of the community and offers too little in return. The individual often demands too many items that are meant to be available for the whole community. The individual can demand too much authority over the other members of the community.

The community on its part can demand too much of the individual. It can demand inappropriate sacrifices, e.g., the pursuit of an unjust war, or the unjust pressure to move from house and land. It can provide too little of the goods that are means for all the individuals of a community. It can crush the wills of individuals by a process of domination and surveillance. The community can impose on the individual by demanding him or her to give up a legitimate pursuit of the arts and culture (e.g., the control of art and architecture in Nazi Germany). The same kind of disunity can exist between various communities of the world (families, states). States can oppress each other, making it impossible or difficult for them to achieve their legitimate goals of self-development and culture.

Disunity occurs when individuals do not use their life energies to build up and serve the community, when they do not care to be disturbed in their routine, when they are willing to drift. Juan Segundo expresses this condition in terms of entropy and holds that it leads to disintegration: "At the level where love clusters all the energies of the universe for their maximum potentialities we find entropy, almost imperceptible, taking the form of sin, that is, the easy road to egotism and routine that leads to disintegration."[39] Disunity is caused, not just by active infringement on the rights of others, but also by permitting the ties of community to go slack, by allowing the outer-directed energies to dissipate. The diminishment of energy results in the disintegration of the community.

The individual is never able to unite all the forces in a harmonious whole. The tensions within the self, the forces of narcissism, the drive for possessions, the demands of the community—all these are never brought into complete harmony. Unity and integration are always a more-or-less. It is true, however, that some individuals are more successful than others in coordinating the internal and external forces that characterize human existence.

The lack of ultimate integration in self and between self and community brings one to the conclusion that final harmony, if it is to be achieved at all, must come from outside the self and the community.[40] The very power of God is needed to bring about unity.

It is now assumed that the guilt of the first human or humans cannot be passed on as an inheritance: ". . . what brings the sin of a community about is not that the guilt of one person simply passes to another person. That conflicts with the principle of personal responsibility."[41] Guilt is incurred by personal failure. It is a matter of personal responsibility. It is also true that in many respects no one stands alone on this earth. Each person belongs to some community.

God, too, is interested in a people; he calls a whole community. But from another standpoint each person stands alone in the presence of God. Each person receives a call to share the life of God; each person responds in a unique fashion. No two persons hear the word in precisely the same way; no two persons form the sentiments of faith and hope in precisely the same manner; no two persons build up or tear down the human community in precisely the same fashion; no two persons are consciously or unconsciously related to Christ in precisely the same way. The conceptualization of God, Christ, and Church vary from person to person. The understanding of moral duty varies from person to person. The way in which moral action is pursued within the human community varies from person to person. In the last analysis persons are unique, and God regards each person as singular and unrepeatable. A person's actual guilt in any moral failure is ultimately known to God alone. He alone can assess the person's dispositions and potentialities; he alone can weigh the strength of the personal choice and the person's view of the harm.

It is assumed, of course, that a person can be disposed for moral failure by many factors—natural, personal, and communitarian.[42] Here it needs to be stressed that personal responsibility and culpability can be present in spite of and in the face of many factors that influence the decision. Personal accountability remains, and where there is personal failure there is also personal guilt. Each person is responsible for his or her own moral offense, even when circumstances facilitate or deter a specific course of action. The offense of one person cannot be handed on to another person. Each person is a fresh creation, someone who has never existed before, someone who is destined to live a unique life, however short or long.

The symbol of disunity does not deny the presence of moral failure in the world. It expresses the involvement of humans in moral evil. It points to the many offenses that are committed by individuals. But it does not express the transfer of a state of guilt from one person to another.

5. Affective Dimensions of Disunity

The effects of any symbol are not confined to the conceptual or cerebral dimensions of the human person. The symbol sets in motion responses on the affective levels of an individual. It has repercussions on the level of one's sentiments and feelings.

The symbol of disunity produces immediate reactions in the human heart and mind. It casts a shadow over the brightness of human existence. It is especially when one assumes that the whole world is without flaw, or at least that it abides with only minor flaws, that the symbol of disunity is present to express somber dimensions of human life. The symbol causes anxiety, for it draws attention to a dark side of life, even when a person does not wish to attend to such a side. The symbol causes uneasiness, for it expresses the flaw without indicating precisely the depth of the failure. The individual is left to estimate the immensity of the flaw for himself or herself. And since the depth is unfathomable, it causes apprehension.

The symbol is not present in Christian theology to induce moral failure. It is there to express the reality of the human condition, even when the grasp of the symbol does not leave a pleasant feeling. The symbol is a reality indicator, a pointer to the real even if unsounded depths of the human condition. It is not designed to make a person feel good, but to express theologically, doctrinally, and experientially the shape of the human condition.

The symbol of disunity has the power to induce emotional responses in those who perceive its symbolic expression. It is difficult to remain unmoved in the face of this symbol. The symbol draws the person to look more closely at the underlying reality of fault and failure. It induces agony over the human condition. As it calls attention to the depths of human brokenness, the symbol produces mixed emotions of discouragement, anger, resignation, and fear. There is discouragement with the failure that pervades human existence and that seems to perpetuate itself. There is anger that a failure beyond one's control reaches personal life and affects it to the core of its being. There is sad resignation to the condition which pre-exists one's birth and life and which seems incapable of amelioration. There is fear that the condition of failure will eventually overcome the self as it has overcome many persons in the past. In short, the symbol is able to bring about an emotional response in those who perceive it and who allow it to enter their life.

6. Disunity as Sinful Disposition

Today disunity is experienced as an inclination to sin, as a disposition to sin. It is not just that "opportunities" for sin are always at hand, that many factors exterior to the person press in upon human life and lead one to the brink of moral failure; it is also the fact that the person perceives an inner proclivity toward evil. There is also a proclivity toward the good, but here there is discussion of an opposite (even if not equal) inclination to sin.

Traditional theology used the word "concupiscence" to express this inclination to sin. Theologians varied in their appraisal of the nature and extent of concupiscence. Concupiscence was the human desire for the sinfully immoderate. It ranged from intellectual desires to bodily appetites such as those of riches or sex. Often it was regarded primarily as inordinate sexual desire, or rather, the most evident experience of concupiscence was felt to be in the realm of sexual desire. In any event, the bodily dimension was always associated with the concept of concupiscence, even when there was question of spiritual or mental desires.

Saint Augustine stressed the role of concupiscence in original sin. His name is often associated with the physical or even sexual dimension of original sin. Some interpreters believe that Augustine defined original sin in terms of concupiscence, that for him original sin is concupiscence. Vandervelde, for instance, holds that for Augustine original sin is in some way identified with concupiscence.[43] But others hold that he did not make such an identification.[44] Alfred Vanneste, however, holds that it is still a disputed question whether or not Augustine identified concupiscence and original sin.[45]

Thomas Aquinas clearly relegates concupiscence to the material element of original sin.[46] Using the Aristotelian terminology of the four causes, Thomas sees the formal element of original sin in the loss of original justice, in the absence of sanctifying grace and friendship with God. The concupiscence that remains in the descendants of Adam, even after the reception of baptism, constitutes only the material element of original sin.

Martin Luther seemed to identify concupiscence and original sin,[47] but, on the contrary, his definition of concupiscence is very broad. Concupiscence is not just the evil inclination in the human body or spirit; it is also and even primarily the hatred of God. For Luther the one term "concupiscence" includes the whole range of inordinate desires and of oppositions to God.

The Council of Trent responded to the Protestant reformers by declaring that concupiscence is *not* sin. It is present in the human body because of sin, in particular because of the sin of Adam that resulted in the removal of the preternatural gifts. As a temptation and inclination, it leads to sin. And at times it may even be called sin. But in actuality it is not sin.

The teaching of Trent prevailed in Roman Catholic circles until recently, though there were theological attempts to re-interpret the meaning of concupiscence. Karl Rahner's suggestion may serve as an example. In an article published over twenty years ago he proposed three senses of the word concupiscence: 1) a broad sense—the simple appetite of the senses and of the spirit; deliberate or indeliberate desires that reach for the good or repudiate the unsuitable; 2) a narrow sense—the indeliberate or spontaneous act of desire; and 3) a technical, theological sense—spontaneous acts of desire that oppose free decision, that hinder the desire for good or evil; it is essentially sluggishness in the pursuit of good or evil.[48]

The traditional term "concupiscence" often left people with the impression that the basic human desires or appetites are tainted in themselves. The word concupiscence was often connected with the idea of original sin as a physical taint of nature, as a defilement of nature that was passed on with the acts of generation and birth. It was assumed that the basic desires continued to afflict the human person even after the reception of baptism. In general, concupiscence was regarded as an unfortunate and tainted aspect of the human body/spirit, something to contend with until death.

There was, of course, much truth in the traditional concept of concupiscence. But unfortunately the teaching on concupiscence left the impression that there was a basic taint in human nature. Today a doctrine of sin as disunity attempts to retain the notion of an inclination to sin without the accompanying assumption of a basically tainted nature. Today disunity is experienced as a disposition to sin, an inclination to sin. There is always at hand the possibility of going beyond the proper limits of need and order. There is, it is true, natural and wholesome desire for food, drink and sex. But the desire for nourishment can incline a person to sin if he or she seeks the kind of food and drink that is harmful to personal health, seeks it in such delicate quality and massive quantity that others are deprived of needed sustenance. The wholesome sexual desire can lead to marital commitment and offspring, but it can also lead to the oppression of the other person through rape and domination. The legitimate desire for a place of one's own can lead to the exclusion of the needs which others have for shelter. The desire for the latest in cars, TV's, and vacation trips can cause others to go in want. The wholesome desire for recognition and acceptance can lead a person to manipulate, to oppress, and to neglect others.

There is a sense in which the legitimate desires of the human body/ spirit can be allowed fulfillment beyond need and order. The word "order" is included because the fulness of human life is pursued beyond the barest needs. There is an order to desire that goes beyond basic needs and ensures a fuller development of human life—body, mind, and spirit. The development of a rose garden, for instance, goes beyond basic needs but contributes to the enhancement of human life, one's own and that of others.

Today Christian theology stresses an aspect of human life that was always held as a matter of doctrine but somewhat compromised by a concept of a tainted nature. It is the basic goodness of human life, a theme that is present in the first chapter of Genesis and continues through the history of the Bible and the Church. Human life is basically good; its core desires are good. But why, then, is there moral evil, moral failure, and disunity? Why is there inclination, not only to the proper aims of one's desires, but also to the inordinate and the sinful? The structure of the human person, while good from the aspect of creation, even evolutionary creation, contains dispositions and inclinations which lead to moral fault. Here it is argued that there are inclinations leading to moral failure, that the disorder is always at hand waiting for the willful approval of the human person.

7. Disunity as Self-Centeredness

On July 20, 1978, NBC-TV presented a special report called "We Want It All Now." It dealt with the style of life of the people of Marin County, California. The report focused in particular on the people's search for pleasure and self-fulfillment. They seemed to be looking for an earthly paradise where every pleasure would be accorded them with abundant ease. They were seeking to please themselves, and they seemed to have little or no concern for others—husband/wife, children, community. "Let them be responsible for themselves, let them take care of themselves"— such was the drift of their conversations. A shopping mall's store called the "Pleasure Principle" captured the theme of the report and perhaps the goal of the county's people. One got the impression that the whole community, the whole county, was taking a narcissistic trip to pleasure and forgetfulness. Yet at the end of the program there was an interview with one couple that was moving away from the county. Their specific reason was the search for the other, for something or someone beyond themselves, for togetherness, for the enjoyment of children, for seeing another kind of beauty in life.

The Narcissus of Greek mythology saw his reflection in a pool of water and promptly fell in love with his own image. The youth pined away in love for himself and was turned into a flower. There is an aspect of the myth that is true and that captures a dimension of the human spirit. It is the aspect of self-love, a subject that appears not only in myth but also in the writings of philosophers, psychologists, and novelists.

Self-love is described in psychoanalytic literature as narcissism. Otto Kernberg, for instance, describes the main characteristics of narcissistic personalities as "grandiosity, extreme self-centeredness, and a remarkable absence of interest in and empathy for others in spite of the fact that they are so very eager to obtain admiration and approval from other people."[49] Narcissism is a centering on self with gratification and admiration. Freud holds that narcissism is the withdrawal of libidinous interest in the other and a direction of it to self.[50] Narcissism charactizes the movements of infants. The whole of life as they experience it centers on themselves; they demand the attention of others, particularly mothers or mother substitutes, for the needs of food, warmth and closeness. Their world is small and it is necessarily centered on themselves. It is only with the passage of time that they learn to open up and to go out to another world beyond themselves. They learn that there are other objects and persons in their purview, that these others have a life of their own, that these others are not going to meet every demand—at least not immediately— and that needs are fulfilled according to some schedule.

A dimension of narcissistic energy is present throughout one's life. It is even a necessary energy that fosters a healthy respect for the self, but it is always in danger of demanding more than its due.

> These [narcissistic] patients present an unusual degree of self-reference in their interactions with other people, a great need to be loved and admired by others, and a curious apparent contradiction between a very inflated concept of themselves and an inordinate need for tribute from others. Their emotional life is shallow.[51]

There is always the danger of permitting the narcissistic tendency to rule the thoughts and the movements of one's life. The narcissistic tendency must be held in balance with the altruistic tendency, the movement to the other. The person's psychological maturity is measured by the way in which he or she can move out from self in concern for the other, in the creation of goals that are of benefit for others. Narcissism does not conform to the truth, because the world does not center on the self and because the healthy psychological person needs to recognize the legitimate demands of others and to move out of self in community development.

Narcissism is a kind of disunity, for it represents a turning away from others, a turning in upon oneself to the detriment of others. It indicates that one's energy is withdrawn from interest in others and in projects that build up the human community; one's energy is channeled into projects of self-interest. The narcissistic individual places self in the center of life and demands the attention and services of others. He or she is possessed of a self-love that encroaches on the love of others. As Christopher Lasch says, "To live for the moment is the prevailing passion—to live for yourself, not for your predecessors or posterity."[52]

Narcissism points to a psychological structure that allows for the existence of moral failure and that creates a situation of disunity. The tendency of the human person to withdraw interest in others and to focus it on self is the very core of sin, that is, when the tendency is such that it is freely acknowledged and promoted. The person does not create the psychological situation, but the structure is always there ready to be acknowledged. It is a psychological fault which allows for the easy access of moral failure.

Narcissistic self-centeredness is characterized by selfishness. Selfishness is a lack of sharing. The selfish person chooses not to share his or her life with others. He or she clings tightly to possessions: goods and property, talents and ideas. The selfish person surrounds self with the fruits of the earth and centers self in the midst of these fruits. The selfish person believes that he or she would lose vital existence if the fruits were shared with others. The possessions have become so much a part of self that they cannot be released without the feeling of self-diminishment: ". . . some of the most intense narcissistic experiences relate to objects; objects, that is, which are either used in the service of the self and of the maintenance of its instinctual investment, or objects which are themselves experiences as part of the self."[53]

The selfish person deems it necessary to retain possessions in an avaricious manner. The words of the First Letter of John describe well the selfish person: "Carnal allurements, enticements for the eye, the life of empty show—all these are from the world" (1 John 2:16). Included in the "enticements for the eye" is the avaricious desire for the many goods that strike the eye, a desire that surpasses need and measure. Heidegger calls the situation *Verfallenheit*, an enslavement to the things of the world.

Selfishness is not measured by the extent of one's wealth. A wealthy person may be generous or selfish in sharing goods and property. A poor person may be generous or selfish in the use of goods and property. Selfishness is a matter of the heart, the unreadiness to share one's life and goods. It goes beyond the unwillingness to share goods and property. It is especially an unwillingness to share self—to share knowledge, to share living space, to share joy, to share affection.

> The 'original' sin, causing all sorts of troubles, happened the moment a person selfishly refused to share God-given talents and powers with others but, instead, used these gifts against others. This self-centered act of separation refused the trust and dependency so necessary for giving and accepting help, and so kept at a hostile distance the talents intended by God for the enrichment of the entire human family.[54]

Selfishness, like self-centeredness, is inward looking; it is grasping for self; it is retaining for self; it is looking to the furtherance of self at the expense of others. "Since Augustine's profound insights, in Christian theology the selfhood that is closed up within itself and in its worldly possessions has been understood as the real core of sin."[55]

The selfish person does not wish to build up the community, a union of goods and values. He or she seeks to build up self with an entourage of attendants and servants. The self is the center of all people, property, values, and services. The flow of consumption and possession is into self, not into community. Reinhold Niebuhr says rightly that "evil is always the assertion of some self-interest without regard to the whole, whether the whole be conceived as the immediate community, or the total community of mankind, or the total order of the world."[56] The selfish person is interested in community only to the extent that community serves the self. The ultimate motive for any attention to the community is the enhancement of self.

The individual grows up in a community where selfishness is a daily encounter. "I inherited the selfish tendencies of a sinful race, implicit in the very speech I learnt, and impressed by a thousand silent examples."[57] Selfishness is a personal experience but also a community experience. Communities, too, can be selfish and inward looking, rejecting the needs of others and refusing to share goods with them. Families, peoples, and nations can isolate themselves from the needs of the wider human community and selfishly withdraw into themselves. They can seek their own satisfaction, praise, and glory without caring about other communities. As the world becomes more aware of its many peoples and nations, such selfishness becomes more noticeable and reprehensible.[58]

Selfish persons or communities fail to provide for the next generation. They use the fruits of the earth in an extravagant manner, not caring that the next generation will suffer want or ill-fortune because of present misuse of the earth. The energy crisis is a case in point. Is it proper for people today to disturb the land with abandon to get coal for present use, to build more nuclear reactors and to complicate the problem of waste disposal for the future generations, to deplete oil reserves? Obviously these are complicated problems but the question of failing the next generation must be asked. Selfish persons are wasters of the goods of the earth.

Self-centeredness also results from an assumed self-sufficiency. It is a patent untruth that anyone is completely self-sufficient, unassisted by the attentions and encouragements of others. Self-sufficiency, according to Reinhold Niebuhr, is one form of the basic sin: "The ideal of individual self-sufficiency, so exalted in our liberal culture, is recognized in Christian thought as one form of the primal sin. For self-love, which is the root of all sin, takes two social forms. One of them is the domination of the other life by the self. The second is the sin of isolationism."[59]

The extreme form of self-centeredness is the exclusion of God from the conscious center of self. The untruth of self-centeredness is most poignant when the person puts God at a distance from self and regards self as the center of the universe.[60] It is untruth because basically the human person cannot force God to withdraw from his immanence in the world. The human person can refuse to recognize the centrality of God's power and presence, but the refusal does not force God to retreat from the cosmos.

In one sense, however, the self-centered person can make God withdraw from his place of honored presence. Self-centeredness does not allow God to be enthroned in the center of the mind and heart. God is not allowed the scope that is his due. He is not consciously placed in the core of one's being, even though his sustaining power makes it possible for everything to exist.

Self-centeredness results in an isolation from God. Loneliness is already "The human experience of the dark side of God."[61] But self-centeredness increases the loneliness, for it chooses to separate itself from the most significant Other in the universe. It is a breaking of communion with the very focus of all that exists. It is making God inaccessible to self by placing self in the center of one's life and action. Self-centeredness inverts the very order of the universe; it reverses the divine pattern in which God is of necessity the origin and center of all existence.

Put in the most serious moral terms, self-centeredness is self-idolatry. It is the placing of self in the center of existence precisely for the sake of worshipping self. All honor and glory are given to self. All religious attention is directed to the idol of self. Self-centeredness, when it has reached its term, creates a god in its own image and falls down in worship before it.

Self-centeredness is the root of evil.[62] Yet there is a sense in which the self is the center of the universe: the universe of the galaxies and the universe of belief. In one sense the individual is an irreplaceable unit who looks out upon the universe as his or her planet, galaxy, and cosmos. There is a sense in which the whole exists for the self, the whole feeds into the self, the whole is there for the enhancement of the self. The individual cannot make it be otherwise. It is simply a fact that a thinking and willing individual has emerged on this planet earth, finds himself or herself separate from others, and makes his or her way in the flux of life. In one sense the individual exists in awesome isolation, never entirely understood or understanding.

There is also a sense in which the individual believer is a unit in the community of the Church. The individual has come to the point of belief in the midst of a community of persons. The individual is irreplaceable. The communitarian dimensions of the Church—its oneness in Christ, its power in the Holy Spirit, its life for the Father, its communion in gifts —cannot extinguish the uniqueness of the individual. Each believer looks out through his or her own eyes upon a community of believers. The believer finds it impossible to persevere or develop in attachment to Christ without the sustaining power of the community. Yet the individual believer remains wrapped in the inviolability of his or her own personhood. In a sense the community exists for the individual believer. It is the individual believer that loves Christ, that seeks eternal life in his name and power.

From another standpoint, however, the individual exists in this universe because of the power of the universe. Life and power stream from the universe and from the phylum of life to bring existence to the individual.

Self-centeredness is the core of sin. It is the very origin of sin and the extreme of disunity. All aspects of moral failure stem from an improper relationship to self. Every sin against God and others begins with a self-centeredness that refuses to allow a bridge to be built between self and others, or permits only a defective bridge. Every sin is the refusal of the proper recognition of the other person, not allowing him or her room in life, not permitting him or her the possibilities of development.

Self-centeredness means that one's interest is directed to self. Assuredly, there is an appropriate interest in self which everyone is obliged to develop. One can develop one's mental and physical capabilities only by proper attention to the self, by taking thought for the preservation and unfolding of one's gifts. There is surely a legitimate interest in self that is required by the very character of life as a gift. One is happy with the personal life that is a gift of God and of the forces of the cosmos.

But there is an interest in self-development and self-preservation which goes beyond the proper measure. It is the kind that seeks self interests to the detriment of other persons and their interests. One claims for self an excessive amount of the fruits of the earth for personal development: excessive travel funds and energy; excessive time and materials for recreation. Or one imposes excessively on others for the development of one's own mind and artistic talents. One may demand of others money, energy, time, and materials to develop self, and the demand may create a real hardship on them (e.g., on wife or husband, children, relatives, state). One demands the right to develop one's talents to their fullest, even to the point of causing others to neglect their gifts and talents. One insists that others make available their own time and energy for the development of one's life. One places oneself in the center of all interest and demands service of others. It is not only a neglect of the interests of others but a demand that they recognize one's interest as supreme and all-encompassing.[63]

One can also pursue self-interests that are devious, e.g., a political leader's desire for dominance. Governors can wish to be the center of attraction to the point of requiring others to serve them. They can wish for or even gain the power to impose a way of life on others. They can find satisfaction in the realization that others are hemmed in by their orders, that they are not able to live their lives freely but must always consider the demands of the dictator. The dictator becomes the center of all attention and activity. All lines of authority and all essential movements in a realm focus on the dictator. The fault here is the desire to make self the center of interest and power to the point where others are hindered in their self-development and well-being.

Besides the political leader the business manager can be one who looks out only for himself or herself, who pushes others out of the way in order to reach the top, who is interested only in his or her own success as a business person. Robert Bellah describes people of this sort when he says:

> This new middle class believes in the gospel of success 1980 style. It is an ethic of how to get ahead in the corporate bureaucratic world while maximizing one's private goodies. In the world of the zero sum society it is important to get to the well first before it dries up, to look out for number one, to take responsibility for your own life and keep it, while also playing the corporate game.[64]

Self-glorification is a form of self-centeredness. In self-glorification the person seeks the praise of self either through one's own expression or through the words and actions of others. The person seeks praise and adulation. His or her whole effort is to think and to act in such a way as to draw attention to self.[65] Great feats are undertaken for the purpose of gaining the praise of others. Even great works of benefit for humankind (scientific discoveries, political achievements) are pursued for the sake of the glory that comes as a reward of one's efforts. It is true, of course, that a person's motives for pursuing science or politics can be, and generally are, multiple. But it is very easy to select the self-glorification motive as foremost. In any event, even when altruistic motives are in the forefront, the dimension of self-glorification is at least minimally present. It can easily develop into the guiding motive.

It is well known that an acceptance of self is a prerequisite of good mental health. Self-glorification is not the same as a realistic appraisal of one's gifts and of the possibility of their development. The self-glorification at issue here is not dishonesty with regard to the values and virtues of the self. The self-centeredness considered here is the continual and never satisfied drive for praise and glory. It is the pursuit of the award, the word of praise, the expression of adulation. Praise is sought even when it is undeserved. The glorification of self becomes the sole motive for living and acting. The self is centered in its own glory.

Is there something about personal human existence that requires self-glorification? Can we live without it? Would life be possible without it? Is it so closely attached to an honest and proper appraisal of self and an open acceptance of merited praise that it is always present, or rather that its possibility is always present? Reinhold Niebuhr, while noting the inevitability of self-love, proposes the paradox that it is not naturally necessary: "The Christian doctrine of original sin with its seemingly contradictory assertions about the inevitability of sin and man's responsibility for sin is a dialectical truth which does justice to the fact that man's self-love and self-centeredness is inevitable, but not in such a way as to fit into the category of natural necessity."[66] Merited praise slides easily into self-glorification and the search for adulation. The origin of sin lies in the capacity of the person to seek acceptance to the point of self-glorification. The true acceptance of self is surpassed to the point where motivation becomes centered in the self—a centering which brings with it a diminution of the going out of the person to others.

8. Disunity and Grace

The existence of a creation that is not God introduces a certain dividedness. God is not created being and created being is not God. The distance between God and creation remains a constant. This is especially true of human creation. In the words of Kenneth Burke, "the possibility of a 'Fall' is implied in the idea of Creation, insofar as the Creation was a kind of 'divisiveness,' since it set up different categories of things which could be variously at odds with one another and which accordingly lack the proto-Edenic simplicity of absolute unity."[67] Dividedness here does not mean that creation is evil; it merely means that creation is the substructure of possibility of a moral rift between God and humans.

The basic dividedness is the distance between God and humans. In a certain sense this distance cannot be overcome. God cannot cease to be God, even assuming the event of the Incarnation. Nor can humans cease to be human, even assuming a divinization. Not at issue here is the way in which the Son of God becomes man and assumes a human dimension. It is a doctrine of faith that the Word of God is enfleshed in human existence without ceasing to be in the realm of the Father. Further, not at issue here is the promise of eternal life expressed in the good news of the New Testament. It is Christian doctrine that humans will enjoy a life with God (indeed they enjoy such a life already), but the sharing in the divine life will not convert humans into God himself. Such an eschatological sharing in the divine life overcomes the painful separateness of God and humans, but it cannot turn humans into God or God into humans.

The extreme form of disunity is rebellion against God. The greatest distance between God and the human person obtains when there is a conscious opposition to God. The individual chooses and fosters disunity for a variety of reasons, the principal one of which is pride. In pride the human person can exclude God from the center of his or her existence and place self in his stead. Disunity may also take the form of rejection of God's word, his ways, his call, his gracious approach.

While rebellion may be the extreme in distance between God and humans, disunity is patient of many degrees. Disunity may be characterized as a lack of belief in God, though this does not exclude an unconscious and implicit attachment to God. It may be marked as a sluggishness in response to God's word and ways. It may be operative as an uncertainty about what God requires. The point at issue here is dividedness between God and humans as the maximum expression of disunity.

The symbol of disunity indicates that humans remain basically powerless in the presence of a God who calls them to a life with himself. Humans cannot bridge the gap that yawns between God and themselves, even when God reveals that the gap should be spanned. God himself must provide the call and the bridge. He himself creates the bridge and makes it possible for humans to travel the distance between the divine and the human. The crossing, of course, requires the willingness of humans to make the journey. The bridge is provided by God, but the crossing implies human cooperation.

To continue the image of the bridge, Christ is the essential *pontifex*, the bridge and the bridge builder. As Son of God the Father, Christ spans the distance between the lordship of God and the lowliness of humans. He includes in his person both exaltedness and emptiness. He is the personal embodiment of the way which leads from the side of humans to the realm of God. No one comes to the Father except through the person of Jesus, the Christ. In him all things have their consistency and hold together. In him there is a creation that is already directed to a union of the human and the divine.

When persons come into existence, they find themselves in this situation: they are called to share the life of God both in the present world and in a life beyond death. The call is itself a grace. It is a gracious favor of God to call humans to share his life. Thus, from this standpoint (and others) humans never come into this world in a graceless situation. Humans have a basic orientation to life with God, an orientation that characterizes their very structure and that is present whether they acknowledge it or not, whether they accept it or not. It is a prepersonal disposition of the human being in the face of a gracious God. It is assumed here that Christians have come to understand the depths of this orientation only through the person of Jesus Christ. This gracious favor of God becomes manifest in Jesus, who is the light of everyone in the world (John 1:9).

There are many other graceful situations that characterize the human person as he or she comes into the world. There is the advantage of being born into a family where love and integrity are upheld. There is the grace of being received and loved by a Church community. There is the abiding presence of the Holy Spirit.

These are a few graces that enfold a person as he or she comes into existence. There is never a situation which is so graceless that it is untouched by God in Jesus Christ and their Spirit. There are many graces and favors that are of divine creation, and they are not the personal fabrication of the individual who comes into human existence. The graces cannot be manufactured. They are simply given; they are the result of divine beneficence. The human person can only stand in grateful reception of these favors.

The symbol of disunity points to the fact that humans are implicated in moral failure. They fail themselves by refusing to develop the potentialities that they receive from birth. Each person receives gifts of mind and body, gifts that are never exactly comparable to those of another person. Each person is responsible for the development of his or her powers of life. But where there is responsibility, there is also the possibility of failure. Moral failure occurs when a person either refuses to develop the givens of existence or does so in a sluggish fashion. Failure to develop oneself, of course, is not always a matter of personal responsibility. Historical and environmental, sociological and psychological factors always situate the individual's decisions, assisting or hindering the cause of development. It is sufficient to note here that it is possible for a person to fail himself or herself and thus to create disunity between potentialities and actualities, between vocation and response.

It is also a fact that people fail each other and cause disunity in social relationships. A cursory reading of the newspaper yields daily examples of the way in which people fail each other: military oppression, governmental graft, editorial untruth, murderous violence. The variety of ways in which people fail each other in the human community defies exhaustive enumeration and seems to increase from age to age. Not in contention here is the fact that many of these failures are beyond the pale of moral responsibility. Surely not all of them stem from willful and deliberate moral action. But, on the other hand, not all of them are determined by circumstances of nature and environment. Many come about because people willingly choose the harmful action.

It is also a fact that people fail the universe in which they live. They exploit it for their own profit and convenience. They waste it in a measure that exceeds their needs and development. This does not mean, of course, that people can never tamper with the world in which they live. They need to live in a symbiotic relationship with the world, and this relationship results in the use of the earth. It is not the use of the earth that is in question here, but the abuse of the earth: its disregard, its rape, its waste. It is almost impossible to determine the fine line between use and abuse, but it is readily acknowledged that people can abuse the earth willingly and deliberately. Waste of the earth can be a morally culpable act and drive a wedge of disunity between people and their earth.

It is also a fact that people can fail God in a morally culpable fashion. They can explicitly refuse to acknowledge his sustaining presence and his gracious favors. They can refuse to ascribe to him the glory of the universe and the benefits of humankind. This is not to say that everyone who consciously refuses to acknowledge the presence and gifts of God fails morally. Various conditions (familial, societal, philosophical) can conspire to situate one's approach to God; these conditions can augment or eliminate a moral response to God. But the point here is that it is possible to disregard love for God and a response to his call. It is possible for humans to turn away from their basic orientation to God and to his call. It is the awful situation of humans that they can turn away from God in a fashion that entails moral failure and disunity.

The symbol of disunity refers to the dimension of moral failure that exists in the human community. The symbol indicates that it is not only possible for people to fail the God who calls them, the universe that sustains them, the community that nourishes them, the self that supports them; it indicates that such a fissure of disunity has in fact taken place, that it does take place, and that it will take place in the future.

While it is true that the situation of humans is never entirely graceless, it is also true that the situation is never without some form of disunity. Moral failures go back in time to the origin of the human species. Moral failure is one of the characteristics of human life. Within a total description of humankind the situation of moral failure has to be included. This is not to propose that disunity is the basic disposition of humans or that disunity lies at the very root of what it is to be human. The corruption of the human heart is not the central feature of the human being. But it would be inaccurate to hold that the human person is only slightly touched by a brush with moral evil. Moral evil penetrates the whole of human existence and causes a division within the very heart of the individual. It drives a wedge between the more basic orientations of humans: their orientation toward God, toward the proper use of the earth, toward the upbuilding of the human community, toward the development of self.

The symbol of disunity points to the divisions that occur responsibly in the human world. It is the theological way of saying that dividedness is present in the world, in the human community, and in the human heart. It is a dividedness that itself calls for revision and reconciliation.

The disunity in the human heart and in the human community calls for reconciliation. The symbol of disunity points to the divided human condition and the need for reconciliation. It can only point, it cannot demand reconciliation. In Christian theology the work of reconciliation is effected in Christ, the mediator between God and humankind. Forgiveness of sins, the overcoming of real moral failure takes place in him. He is the bridge that overcomes the moral distance between the sinful human condition and the gracious God. Forgiveness of sin is the grace that most directly attends to the human condition characterized by the symbol of disunity. The symbol points to the division in the heart of humans, a division that receives its elimination in the forgiveness offered by Christ in the presence of his Spirit.[68]

9. Summary of Chapter II

Original sin is theology's traditional symbol of the human condition that is described as a rebellion against God, a proneness to evil, pride and self-exaltation, and a certainty of death. In this second chapter, I have pointed up the deficiencies of the theological symbol of original sin and have suggested the symbol of disunity as more appropriate. The symbol of disunity adequately discloses the multiple aspects of conflict and dividedness in the human situation. As an integrative symbol, disunity brings together and expresses the many divisions that characterize human existence on this earth.

Disunity gives verbal form to the moral distance that one experiences between self and God. It is not just that creation is ontologically distinct from God but also that the human person puts self ahead of God and rises up in rebellion against him.

Moral distance from God is the maximum of disunity but it is symptomatic of other conflicts of human existence. There is also the disunity that is experienced when one community oppresses another, one nation destroys another, one society dominates another. There is also the disunity that one experiences when he or she wastes the goods of the world or refuses to develop created potentialities.

The deepest rift of disunity, however, is formed in the human heart when the self turns away from others in selfishness and self-sufficiency.

Self-centeredness not only disrupts the relationship to God but also destroys the true values of self in relation to community and world. Narcissistic living results in loneliness and confusion because it ignores community and the proper order of the universe. Self-centeredness reaches its maximum point of disunity when the individual begins to glorify self, when he or she establishes self as the adorable center of all existence.

Humans in the world find themselves in various phases of disunity. They are born into this condition and they confirm it in various ways by a life that is devoted, at least partially, to disjunctive self-centeredness. Disunity is the human condition that calls out for redemption, a reaching for community.

Footnotes

CHAPTER 2

[1] *Religious Experience and Truth: A Symposium,* ed. Sidney Hook (New York: New York University Press, 1961), pp. 3-11.

[2] *Ibid.,* p. 4.

[3] *Ibid.,* p. 5.

[4] *Ibid.,* p. 5.

[5] "Theology and Symbolism," *Religious Symbolism,* ed. F. E. Johnson (New York: Harper and Brothers, 1955), p. 110.

[6] *Religious Symbols and God: A Philosophical Study of Tillich's Theology* (Chicago: University of Chicago Press, 1968), p. 101.

[7] See "Theology and Symbolism" p. 112; *Systematic Theology,* Vol. II, pp. 88-96.

[8] *Dynamics of Faith* (New York: Harper Torchbooks, 1958), p. 49.

[9] See David M. Rasmussen, *Symbol and Interpretation* (The Hague: Martinus Nijhoff, 1974), p. 4.

[10] Boston: Beacon Press, 1969.

[11] *Freud and Philosophy: An Essay on Interpretation* (New Haven, Conn.: Yale University Press, 1970), p. 9.

[12] See *The Symbolism of Evil,* pp. 10-18.

[13] D. Idhe says that this aphorism derives from Kant: *Hermeneutic Phenomenology,* p. 99.

[14] David Tracy praises the vital notion of symbol in the thought of Paul Ricoeur: "The most influential notion of 'symbol' in modernity remains Kant's notion of those re-presentations in which imagination 'binds up' or concentrates so many ideas that they 'arouse more thought than can be expressed in a concept determined by words.' Clearly this conception of symbol as re-presentation remains operative in philosophical works like Paul Ricoeur's *Symbolism of Evil. ...*" *The Analogical Imagination: Christian Theology and the Culture of Pluralism* (New York: The Seabury Press, 1981), p. 108, note 36.

[15] *The Symbolism of Evil,* p. 18. The myth is "a form of narration: it recounts the events of the beginning and the end inside a fundamental time...." So Ricoeur states in *The Conflict of Interpretations: Essays in Hermeneutics.* Edited by D. Ihde (Evanston: Northwestern University Press, 1974), p. 28.

[16] Cf. *The Symbolism of Evil,* pp. 3-24.

[17] p. 12.

[18] *Ibid.,* p. 289.

[19] See the Preface in D. Ihde, *Hermeneutic Phenomenology,* pp. xvi-xvii.

[20] "Structure, Word, Event," *Philosophy Today* 12 (1968) p. 126.

[21] Alasdair MacIntyre and Paul Ricoeur, "Religion, Atheism, and Faith," *The Religious Significance of Atheism* (New York: Columbia University Press, 1969), p. 98.

[22] "Structure, Word, Event," p. 127.

[23] *Interpretation Theory: Discourse and the Surplus of Meaning* (Forth Worth: Texas Christian University Press, 1976), p. 45.

[24] See A. Vanneste, "Où en est le problème du péché originel?" *Ephemerides Lovanienses*, 52 (1976), p. 146.

[25] *On Marriage and Concupiscence*, Bk. II, Chap. 12, 25 (CSEL 42, 278).

[26] Cited by Paul Althaus, *The Theology of Martin Luther* (Philadelphia: Fortress Press, 1966), p. 240, note 76.

[27] *Preface to the Epistle of St. Paul to the Romans*. See *Martin Luther: Selections From His Writings*. Edited and with an Introduction by John Dillenberger (Garden City, New York: Doubleday & Co., Anchor Books, 1961), pp. 22-23.

[28] DS 370-397.

[29] DS 398-400. See J. Redding, *The Influence of Saint Augustine on the Doctrine of the II Council of Orange Concerning Original Sin* (Washington, D.C.: The Catholic University of America, 1939).

[30] See Heiko Oberman, "Facientibus quod in se est Deus non denegat gratiam: Robert Holcot, O.P., and the Beginnings of Luther's Theology," *Harvard Theological Review*, 55 (1962), pp. 317-342.

[31] See Canon 1.

[32] Canon 2.

[33] Canons 3 and 4.

[34] Canon 5.

[35] A. Vanneste, "Le dogme de l'Immaculée Conception et l'evolution actuelle de la théologie du péché originel," *Ephemerides Mariologicae*, 23 (1973), p. 89. A. Schmied, "Konvergenzen in der Diskussion um die Erbsünde," *Theologie der Gegenwart*, 17 (1974), p. 149.

[36] See Z. Alszeghy and M. Flick, "What did Trent define about Original Sin," *Theology Digest*, 21 (1973), p. 63.

[37] *Ibid.*, p. 65.

[38] Art. 13. *Vatican Council II: The Conciliar and Post Conciliar Documents*. Edited by Austin Flannery, O.P. (Collegeville, Minn.: The Liturgical Press, 1975), p. 914.

[39] *Evolution and Guilt* (Maryknoll, N.Y.: Orbis Press, 1974), p. 108.

[40] Cf. Wolfhart Pannenberg, *What is Man? Contemporary Anthropology in Theological Perspective* (Philadelphia: Fortress Press, 1970), p. 63.

[41] P. Schoonenberg, *Man and Sin*, p. 103.

[42] See Chapter 1.

[43] *Original Sin. Two Major Trends in Contemporary Roman Catholic Reinterpretation* (Amsterdam: Rodopi, 1975), p. 16. See also Henri Rondet, *Original Sin. The Patristic and Theological Background* (Staten Island, N.Y.: Alba House, 1972), p. 143.

[44] G. Daly, for instance, denies the identification: "Theological Models in the Doctrine of Original Sin," *The Heythrop Journal*, 13 (1972), p. 126. See also E. TeSelle, *Augustine the Theologian* (New York: Herder and Herder, 1970), pp. 317-18. See as well Leo Scheffczyk, *Urstand, Fall und Erbsünde. Von der Schrift bis Augustinus* (Freiburg: Herder, 1981), pp. 212-229.

[45] "Le préhistoire du décret de Concile de Trente sur le péché originel," *Nouvelle Revue Théologique*, 86 (1964), p. 499, note 105.

[46] *Summa Theologiae*, I-II, q. 82, a.3.

[47] G. Daly thinks he did identify concupiscence and original sin: "Theological Models in the Doctrine of Original Sin," p. 126.

[48] "The Theological Concept of Concupiscence," *Theological Investigations,* Vol. I (Baltimore: Helicon, 1961), pp. 347-382.

[49] *Borderline Conditions and Pathological Narcissism* (New York: Jason Aronson, Inc., 1975), p. 228.

[50] See Erich Fromm, *The Anatomy of Human Destructiveness* (New York: Holt, Rinehart and Winston, 1973), p. 200.

[51] O. Kernberg, *Borderline Conditions and Pathological Narcissism*, p. 17.

[52] *The Culture of Narcissism: American Life in an Age of Diminishing Expectations* (New York: W. W. Norton & Co., 1978), p. 5.

[53] H. Kohut, *The Analysis of the Self* (New York: International Universities Press, 1971), p. xiv.

[54] C. Stuhlmueller, C.P., "Repentance for Original Sin and Reconciliation in Christ," *Communio*, 1 (1974), p. 37.

[55] W. Pannenberg, *What is Man?* p. 63.

[56] *The Children of Light and the Children of Darkness*, p. 9.

[57] A. Farrer, *Love Almighty and Ills Unlimited* (Garden City, N.Y.: Doubleday, 1961), p. 135.

[58] "Group-egoism, which arises from self-preservation and leads to struggles for survival and power, threatens mankind with collective suicide today." So states Jürgen Moltmann, "Hope and the Biomedical Future of Man," *Hope and the Future of Man*, ed. by E. H. Cousins (Philadelphia: Fortress Press, 1972), p. 98.

[59] *The Children of Light and the Children of Darkness*, p. 55.

[60] Sebastian Moore says: "The experience of original sin is produced by the withdrawing of the self from its primordial leanings toward ultimate mystery into absolute isolated selfhood." *The Fire and the Rose are One* (New York: Seabury Press, 1980), p. 67.

[61] John Dunne, *The Reasons of the Heart. A Journey into Solitude and Back Again into the Human Circle* (New York: Macmillan, 1978), p. 81.

[62] D. J. Jenkins suggests that there is no point in looking for a cause of self-centeredness; it is simply a fact of the situation. See "Responsibility, Freedom and the Fall," E. Kemp, *Man: Fallen and Free* (London: Hodder and Stoughton, 1969), p. 28. As I am describing the situation, however, I wish to note some predisposing factors that make self-centeredness possible.

[63] See Reinhold Niebuhr: "The children of darkness are evil because they know no law beyond the self. They are wise, though evil, because they understand the power of self-interest." *The Children of Light and the Children of Darkness*, p. 10.

[64] "Religion and Power in America Today," in *Proceedings of the Catholic Theological Society of America*, 37 (1982), p. 19.

[65] Cf. C. Lasch, "All of us, actors and spectators alike, live surrounded by mirrors. In them, we seek reassurance of our capacity to captivate or impress others, anxiously searching out blemishes that might detract from the appearance we intend to project." *The Culture of Narcissism*, p. 92.

[66] *The Nature and Destiny of Man* (New York: C. Scribner's Sons, 1949), p. 263.

[67] K. Burke, "On the First Three Chapters of Genesis," ed. R. May, *Symbolism in Religion and Literature*, p. 119.

[68] See the suggestion of A. Vanneste, who describes original sin in terms of the need for Christ and his forgiveness since everyone is either an actual sinner or a virtual sinner (that is, a child sins when it reaches the age of reason): *Le Dogme du Péché Originel* (Louvain: Éditions Nauwelaerts, 1971), p. 141. See also H. Haag:

"Mankind under the power of sin (*amartia*: Rom. 5:12f., 20f.) is mankind outside of Christ; mankind under the power of grace (*charis*: Rom. 5:15, 17, 20f.) is mankind in Christ. It can thus be said that the Catholic doctrine of original sin is nothing other than an attempt to describe theologically the situation of mankind outside of Christ." *Is Original Sin in Scripture?* (New York: Sheed and Ward, 1969), p. 74.

Chapter 3

Community: The Symbol of Grace

Chapter 3 of this book is designed to complement the study of the origin of sin (Chapter 1) and especially the discussion of disunity, the symbol of sin (Chapter 2). Community as the symbol of grace is here proposed as the obverse of disunity, the symbol of sin. If sin is characterized by disunity, grace is marked by community. Community is not only the opposite of disunity, but it is also the very agent that overcomes disunity.

It is clear—and Chapters 1 and 2 have brought to light dimensions of the phenomenon—that the world of our experience is burdened with a condition of sin. Sin confronts us on a daily basis, both in ourselves and in the society in which we live. But sin is not the whole story of our human existence. There is also the condition of goodness in our world. There is not only the pursuit of evil and sin but also the pursuit of peace and justice, honesty and truth, love and goodness. There are examples of evil and examples of good. A situation of good prevails right in the midst of the world where sin is manifest. It is our Christian conviction that goodness prevails because of the action of God in Christ's words and deeds. It is understood in this Chapter 3, and mentioned when appropriate, that Christ has overcome the powers of evil, sin, and death, not in the sense that they no longer exist in our world but in the sense that they have radically met defeat in their opposition to Jesus; that they are still allowed to manifest their power, but that ultimately they will be overcome. In fact, they are already being overcome daily. It is precisely this daily overcoming of evil, sin, and death that is the topic of this section of our study. The powers of sin are overcome within the boundaries of communitarian goodness.

1. The Symbol of Community

The word community suggests the opposite of the word disunity. Whereas disunity means separation, division, and opposition, community means togetherness, union, and fellowship. The community is the situation in which people are in contact with each other, are joined with one another, and are brought together. But this description of community does not yet indicate the intentionalities of the community; it does not indicate why people are in close contact with each other. For a broader notion of community we need to turn to anthropology and sociology.

The concept of community bulks large in any overall discussion of sociology. Many dimensions of human living are studied by sociologists within the conceptual parameters of community. The human community is the place where humans interact, strive to solve their problems of living, and create common goals. Sociologists generally define community in terms of a restricted territory and population. They see the community as the place where humans interact on a daily basis, where they live in relative proximity to each other, where they have similar interests and goals, where there is mutual interchange of care and services (farming, manufacturing, government, etc.).[1] The community is a more restrictive concept than that of society or culture. Society tends to be the larger unit of association and interaction, more comprehensive in territory and in political control, the result of the interaction of many communities. Culture is an even wider concept. It can easily extend to many political units (states and countries) and deal more generally with patterns of life, such as language, customs, laws, political structures, and technology. These patterns, of course, extend to the daily life of communities that share the culture.

Sociologists identify many kinds and sizes of community. Communities differ from each other on the basis of intimacy, geography, ethnicity, and political structure. Communities range from the intimacy of a family community to the hugeness of a political community, from the closeness of a friendship community to the extensive bonds of an ethnic community, from the expansiveness of a rural community to the congestion of an urban community, from the commitment of the religious community to the loyalty of a civic community. Within certain degrees and with the allowance of wide margins, it is possible to mark out the boundaries between communities. Communities are identifiable units of a human society, and people tend to find self-identity within the boundaries of a community or of a cluster of communities.

Some writers use the word community in a sense broader than a group of people that interacts on a daily basis in a relatively restricted geographical area. They use the term to refer to groupings of nations and of peoples around the world—indeed, to the whole of humankind. They speak of the community of peoples or the community of nations. Walter Jeffko, for instance, offers this definition of community:

> Any association, regardless of size, in which all of its members care for one another as persons is a community. Consequently, in principle, there is no

restriction in size upon community. Indeed, in my judgment, the ultimate moral ideal and aim is the creation, maintenance and deepening of universal community. In Christian terminology, this would constitute the kingdom of heaven on earth.[2]

There is some reason to use the term in this broad sense, because today communication is such that people are or can be in informational contact with peoples on the other side of the globe. There is day-to-day information about the other inhabitants of the earth; not only information, but also interaction. A crisis in the Mideast or in Indochina affects daily life in the United States of America. Consider, for example, the holding of American hostages by revolutionary students in Iran (1979-1980). It is becoming clear that we live on a small planet and that we are interdependent. The use of the term "world community" captures the sense of this togetherness and interdependence of peoples on the planet earth.[3]

In this study of disunity and community I will on occasion extend the concept of community to the togetherness of peoples throughout the world. I will focus, to be sure, on the community called Church; but I will of necessity refer to the various communities of our human experience, for all of them are human patterns of living and are able to overcome the condition of disunity.

The Christian community, the community of the Church, is the place of togetherness and concern. I will discuss these and other dimensions of the religious community later, in section 4. Here it should be noted that authentic community of any kind is designed to overcome the ill effects of disunity. It is true that God works through the Church in a special manner to overcome the evils of disunity, but his efforts are not confined to the Christian Church. His Spirit is not confined to the visible structures of the Christian community; it is present throughout the world, for it is as far-reaching as the divine desire for the salvation of humans. It is world-wide precisely because God's will for salvation is directed to all peoples. It is our contention that God can and does work through groupings of people that can be called communities, to bring about the end of disunity and the forgiving effects of togetherness. For this reason, our discussion is not confined to the community of the church but extends to the presence of communities throughout the world. The community is one of the basic human associations that God uses to bring people together in mutual concern and conciliation. It should not be surprising that God uses human groups to effect his purposes, for the history of Israel and of Christianity indicates clearly that God uses particular peoples, languages, customs, and events to reveal his presence, power, and purposes.

The religious dimension of the community, or more particularly the religious community itself, is ultimately the place where disunity is overcome. This statement is based on the conviction that the religious dimension of society and of the community is important for the ultimate reconciliation of the individual and his or her natural environment and for the union of peoples in society. The religious tradition critiques the ephemeral goals of society (success or material wealth) and offers an eternal source of truth. This was T. S. Eliot's conviction when he wrote of the idea of a Christian society more than forty years ago: "As political philosophy derives its sanction from ethics, and ethics from the truth of religion, it is only by returning to the eternal source of truth that we can hope for any social organization which will not, to its ultimate destruction, ignore some essential aspects of reality."[4]

It is ultimately the religious community that will provide the goal of unity. This is a traditional Christian conviction that needs to be elaborated here. Wolfhart Pannenberg expresses the issue very clearly: "Since the problem of social unity is finally a religious one, because religion articulates the awareness of the future destiny of man that bridges over the antagonism between individual and society, therefore religion cannot remain, in the long run, an exclusively private concern."[5]

In this study I am considering the unitary effects of the Christian community. I proceed in this way because of my commitment to the Christian tradition as the authentic expression of the divine truth. This does not mean, however, that God is not using other religious traditions to bring about reconciliation and unity among peoples. I acknowledge the unifying effects of the many religious traditions of the world. Surely not every religious tradition is equally successful in this enterprise, but the conviction remains: forces that overcome disunity are present in many religious traditions, even in the midst of obvious failures and deviations (similar to those that exist in the Christian tradition).

A word about the term *communitas* as a verbal symbol. As I indicated above when speaking of symbolism and the symbol of disunity, authors use symbols because of their rich, multidimensional significance. The verbal symbol community has the direct meaning of a unity or a union of persons. But as a rich symbol it points to many other realities associated with the union of persons. It refers to closeness, togetherness, personal relations, mutual understanding, common action and interest, acknowledged goals, freedom, frequent association. The word community can function as a rich symbol because it signifies a concrete reality in the experience of humans, while at the same time it points to a great variety of meaning beyond the literal existence of the community. As such it can function as an appropriate concept to describe the way in which the phenomenon of disunity is overcome in human experience. An elaboration of the significance of *communitas* can point to the richest experience of human living: communitarian sharing in the goods of the earth, association with the peoples of humankind, commitments and joys of community life, fellowship with Christ and his followers, ultimate union with God through an exalted and transcendent experience.

2. The Community of Goods

Disunity is caused to a great extent by the lack of will to share the goods of the earth. Individual and corporate greed is at the basis of much suffering. When greed leads to the appropriation of wealth far beyond need and merit, it creates a division in the human community. The greed of certain individuals, corporations, or nations results in the poverty of other individuals, corporations, or nations; greed brings about disunity in the human community as the have's are set in opposition to the have not's.

It is clear that the goods of the earth are designed for the life and survival of the people of the earth. Humans live on the planet earth and must provide for themselves from the fruits of the earth. They cannot depend on another planet or on divine intervention for their day-to-day survival. They require the daily availability of the gifts of the earth.

These conditions of human life are clear, and they are mentioned here only because they have relevance to the discussion of community. The community of humans is not an ethereal gathering but an association of people rooted in the expansiveness and the limitation of the earth. The human community lives from the goods of the earth and is characterized by its dependence on the fruits of the earth. Earth, territory, and goods enter into the notion of the human community; it cannot be conceived without relation to a common place and shared goods.

The goods of the earth, therefore, precisely because they are required for survival on this planet, are the source of both disunity and community. They are able to split people up into opposing factions; they are able to bring them together into union and community. It is particularly the unifying nature of the goods of the earth that is of interest to us here in our discussion of the sense and direction of community. Goods of the earth have the capacity to bind the community of humans and to help them overcome the evil of disunity.

The fact that the goods of the earth are available for the human community has led many thinkers to postulate a community of goods that would actually be a common ownership of goods. Some thinkers refer to an alleged golden age of the past when humans held goods in common and shared equally in the fruits of the earth. There were early Greek myths, for instance, that referred to a happy and peaceful age of the past when goods were shared in common.

More closely related to the Christian tradition is the practice of the Qumran community, the quasi-monastic group of Jews who separated themselves from the priesthood of Jerusalem a century or more before the time of Christ. They shared a community of goods. Those who joined the community promised to bring "all of their wealth into the community of God, so that . . . their wealth [might be] disposed in accordance with His just design."[6] Their motives for relinquishing their possessions were not always high and noble, if we are to believe the commentary of J. Schattenmann. He claims that the Qumran people turned over their possessions because of "the idea that possession of money was tainted with sin."[7] Important for our purposes is the movement toward a community of goods, even if aspects of the movement are less than wholesome and not in accord with the goodness of creation as depicted in the Genesis account.[8]

Jesus practiced some kind of sharing of goods with his disciples. At least during his period of preaching, he seemed to be quite detached from possessions: "The foxes have lairs, the birds in the sky have nests, but the Son of Man has nowhere to lay his head" (Matt 8:20). Jesus and the disciples, engaged in an itinerant ministry, shared the contributions of benefactors (cf. Luke 8:1-3). The benefactors, women included, not only actively supported the preaching of the gospel but also made it possible for Jesus and the disciples to form a group, a traveling community not dependent upon the incidental alms of passersby. The traveling group also held a common purse (John 12:6; 13:29). Jesus ate and drank with sinners, but he also taught detachment from riches: "Do not lay up for yourselves an earthly treasure. Moths and rust corrode; thieves break in and steal" (Matt 6:19). Jesus and the disciples did not amass an abundance of goods, and they shared the goods that came to them in their ministry. A community of goods was an accompaniment of the community of persons. Disunity entered the scene when dissillusioned Judas appropriated money to himself and complained of the extravagant use of perfume: "Why was not this perfume sold? It could have brought three hundred silver pieces, and the money have been given to the poor. (He did not say this out of concern for the poor, but because he was a thief. He held the purse, and used to help himself to what was deposited there)" (John 12: 5-6).

The primitive Church, as evident in the Acts of the Apostles, held a community of goods in high esteem. It was not a universal practice, but individual believers could donate their goods for common use. The summary statement in chapter 2 proclaims this ideal in a straightforward fashion: "Those who believed shared all things in common; they would sell their property and goods, dividing everything on the basis of each one's need" (Acts 2:44-45; cf. 4:32). But the account of the tragedy that befell Ananias and Sapphira for lying to the Holy Spirit, that is, for pretending to give up all their possessions, indicates that the donation of one's goods to the community was optional: "Was it not yours so long as it remained unsold? Even when you sold it, was not the money still yours?" (Acts 5:4). A person could be a member of the early Christian community without giving up his or her money or property, but believers could and actually did donate their goods. Much property was held in common, and one purpose of the common goods was the assistance that could be offered the needy poor. In this way the early Church continued the Deuteronomic ideal: "There shall be no one of you in need" (Deut 15:4).

The practice of sharing one's goods, especially with the poor, was customary in the early Church. Saint Paul preaches generosity and mentions frequently the collection for the poor Christians of Jerusalem (Acts 24:17; Rom 15:25-31; 1 Cor 16:1-4; 2 Cor 8:1-9:15; Gal 2:10). The collection not only provides the opportunity for a sharing of goods but also strengthens the bonds between the Gentile and the Jewish Christians. This is the point that needs emphasis here. It is precisely the sharing of goods that helps to form community. It is not only a realization that others are needy and have a rightful claim on the goods but also the acknowledgment that sharing links believers in a community of faith. Solidarity is strengthened through a sharing in material goods.

Through the centuries collections have been a regular part of Christian life. The spirit of generosity has certainly waxed and waned from community to community and from age to age, but the principle of sharing continued even when common ownership of lands and buildings was not the regular practice. Kings and governments, it must be remembered, owned many church buildings, and the faithful often did not share in the ownership of the buildings they used.

It was otherwise in monastic and religious orders. Buildings and lands were customarily held in common by the religious community. But this was not always the case. For example, some thirteenth and fourteenth century Franciscans preferred not to own any property and persuaded the pope to hold titles to their lands and buildings. Of course, even in this case the Franciscans shared the goods and property in common, and this is the point we wish to make in this section. Christian faith led these and other religious to share material goods and property. A significant feature of their community life lay in their common use of property. Aside from the vexations that this often entailed—and vexations were never absent from such a practice—the common possession and sharing of goods bonded the community of religious. Fellowship was expressed in the sharing of goods; it was also enhanced and constructed in the sharing of goods. The sharing of goods was itself a voluntary witness to the fact that the goods of the earth are meant to be shared by all the peoples of the earth, and that there should be a common caring to the point of sharing goods and property.

Vatican Council II, in its wide-ranging and forward-looking document called "The Church in the Modern World," reminds us of the community of goods: "God destined the earth and all it contains for all men and all peoples so that all created things would be shared fairly by all mankind under the guidance of justice tempered by charity."[9] The council does not claim that everyone has a right to an identical share in the goods of the earth, but it insists that everyone has a right to a fair share. The council does not dictate a particular method of owning or distributing the goods that people need; it recognizes that many different methods have been and are used in achieving the goal of providing for the needs of the people (clan ownership, private ownership, corporate ownership, etc.). The goods that a person owns, the council continues, can be of benefit for others as well as for oneself. "Therefore every man has the right to possess a sufficient amount of the earth's goods for himself and his family."[10]

It is not our purpose to trace the way in which societal structures have made the goods of the earth available for all peoples, nor the way in which theology has explained the manner of distribution. Our only point is that there is a community of goods, that goods enter into the very structure of the human community, that they firm up the bonds of community even as they provide the source of irritation. It is becoming clearer to us today than it was in the past that the peoples of the world are interrelated, that peoples are more and more dependent on others to acquire the needs of survival and proper existence. It is this realization of the mutual dependence of peoples in the matter of the availability of the goods of the earth that is drawing humankind closer together into one community, or rather, making them realize that they do form one community. The earth and its fullness of goods is drawing tightly the bonds of mutuality and community.

Humankind's necessary dependence on the goods of the earth carries a possible message about the future relationship of humans to the earth. If salvation does not mean escape from the material, if redemption implies a reconciliation of the whole cosmos, it must be stated that the future shape of the human community will always contain a reference to the material, to the cosmos. That the ultimate shape of the human community (see below, section 7) will include a reference to a renewed creation is seen by some commentators in such biblical passages as these: "I mean that God, in Christ, was reconciling the world to himself, not counting men's transgressions against them, and that he has entrusted the message of reconciliation to us" (2 Cor 5:19, cf. Eph 1:10; Rom 8). Or again: "After that will come the end, when after having destroyed every sovereignty, authority, and power, he will hand over the kingdom to God the Father.... When, finally, all has been subjected to the Son, he will then subject himself to the One who made all things subject to him, so that God may be all in all" (1 Cor 15:24, 28). The Son hands over to the Father a universe that is perfectly subject to the divine rule. And again: "It pleased God to make absolute fullness reside in him and, by means of him, to reconcile everything in his person, both on earth and in the heavens, making peace through the blood of his cross" (Col 1:19-20). Christ's death has its effect on the whole of creation, not just on the human community.

The reconciliation of all things in Christ may very well include a renewed relation of the human community to the material cosmos. In this case the community of goods will continue to characterize the transformed community of humankind.

3. The Community of Humankind

If there is a condition of sin and disunity as extensive as the breadth of humankind, there is also a condition of community as wide as the reaches of human existence. The situation of disunity is countered by a movement toward community. Disunity and community characterize peoples the world over both today and in the pages of history. It is the community of peoples and the movements toward world community that I wish to reflect on in this section.

As I noted above, sociologists often view community as the kind of human association that takes place on a day-to-day basis and is confined to a relatively restricted area. But I noted too that the word community can also refer to wider groupings of peoples—the national community, the international community, even the worldwide community. It is the movement toward the worldwide community that is of interest here, though as need arises I will also refer to the smaller communities, especially to the structures that are oriented to the worldwide community.

A theology of the worldwide community brings to mind the universal concern of the God of Israel and the Father of our Lord Jesus Christ. The community of Israel has a special mission to manifest the presence, power, and word of God. The blessing of Abraham is the source of blessings for all nations: "I will make of you a great nation, and I will bless you. . . . All the communities of the earth shall find blessing in you" (Gen 12:2-3). The servant of the Lord, depicted in the book of Isaiah, is a source of light and salvation for all peoples: "I will make you a light to the nations, that my salvation may reach to the ends of the earth" (Isa 49:6). When the people of Israel turned in on themselves after the Babylonian exile, the prophets chided their narrowness and provincialism. The book of Jonah teaches that the Lord God is interested in all peoples.

The gospel of Jesus Christ is also universally directed to all peoples. It is clear from the New Testament that the word of forgiveness, the word of salvation, is oriented to the whole of humankind. The death and the resurrection of Jesus have redemptive significance for every person in the world. All peoples are called to live with God; all are affected by the saving power that is released in the words and deeds of Jesus Christ: "Full authority has been given to me both in heaven and on earth; go, therefore, and make disciples of all the nations" (Matt 28; 18-19).

The radical universality of the Christian gospel, its relation to every individual, is the basis for any theological consideration of a world community. If God does in fact regard the whole of humankind as one beloved people, if he does not selectively reject some groups and elect others, there is reason to reflect theologically on the salvific basis of the world community. There is reason to identify the movements toward world community and to view them in the light of Christian faith.

Today it is much easier to identify the movements toward a world community and to cite their causes. Our scientific knowledge of the place of the earth in the vast universe has led us to see the smallness of our planet. It is one tiny orb in this huge galactic system and is easily encompassed by the human imagination. It is easily viewed in its little wholeness when seen against the backdrop of the expanse of the universe. Humans can easily become overawed by the vastness of the universe and slip into self-defeating musings of insignificance. The opposite reaction to the vastness of the universe is also a possibility; the thought that humans are self-reflective and can understand to some extent their place in this universe is inspiring. In any event, the knowledge of this one small planet teaches humans the unitary character of the world and assists movements toward unity.

The peoples of the world are often regarded as divided into many races. But this division is superficial when compared to the underlying unity of all peoples of the earth. The races of the world are really one human kind, whose differences do not form strict barriers between humans but constitute an asset to the development of the species.

Communication systems (radio, television, telephone, satellite) bring the world into an understanding of its oneness. The interaction of minds has increased phenomenally in the last century. Ideas and knowledge of events are exchanged and transmitted throughout the planet on an ever-increasing scale. What happens on one part of the globe becomes known almost immediately to all parts of the world. There remain, of course, many millions of uninformed and illiterate people on this planet. The literate world is more aware of this fact today than it was in the past. But there is also concern for raising the educational level of all peoples of the world, and this concern constitutes one feature of the movement toward the world community.

In the imagery of Teilhard de Chardin the communication systems of the world have resulted in complexification, a folding in of minds upon themselves. The psychic and communicative energy of the world has increased to the point where individuals may be viewed as cells of an earth brain. The cells remain distinct, but the communication between them has increased and made it possible for the whole to engage in more intensive activity, to think more unitary thoughts, and to build up the earth together. Teilhard de Chardin holds that national boundaries are no longer significant in the work of unifying the forces of the earth: "The resources we enjoy today, the powers and secrets of science we have discovered, cannot be absorbed by the narrow system of individual and national divisions which have so far served the leaders of the world. The age of nations is past. The task before us now, if we would not perish, is to shake off our ancient prejudices, and to build the earth."[11]

Communication between people around the world is not confined to political events and economic matters. It moves into all areas of thought and practice. There is an exchange of scientific information. There is mutual benefit from an exchange of literature, a translation of one country's classic into another's linguistic structures. There is an international community of music, art, and architecture. There is an exchange of values and modes of living. "Thanks above all to an increase in all kinds of interchange between nations the human family is gradually coming to recognize itself and constitute itself as one single community over the whole earth."[12]

Accompanying the phenomenon of communication is the realization of world travel. Modern modes of transportation make it possible for millions of people to visit other countries, to learn their languages, to experience their customs and values, to sample their wares. The unity and diversity of humans become clear to travelers who allow themselves to be exposed to the ways of other peoples.

Economics is another dimension of life that has led to the movement toward the one world community. It is clear today how interdependent peoples are in matters of money, goods, and services. A high form of civilization requires of people the exchange of a great variety of materials, manufactured goods, and services. A highly developed country sustains its level of culture by economic exchange with most other countries of the world. It is obvious, of course, that not all regional peoples have reached the same degree of interdependence and exchange. Some people live in relatively primitive societies, in which they depend very little on outside trade. Some peoples are kept in poverty precisely through exploitation on the part of developed and powerful countries. This unbalanced economic situation is deplorable and can be overcome to some extent by the movement toward world community. Here we only wish to note the movement toward one community of humankind that is driven by economic factors. Economics has manifested the oneness of the human community and is presently acting as a motor to drive the peoples of the world closer together.

The twentieth century has seen many particular movements that lead in the direction of a world community, a community of nations, or at least world cooperation. There are the League of Nations and its post-World War II successor, the United Nations. The goal of the UN falls far short of a world government; but it provides a forum for the nations of the world, and it attempts to foster peace by advocating international cooperation and development. It acknowledges that there are matters that concern every nation: border disputes, atmosphere pollution, world population, etc. In particular it acknowledges the human rights and freedoms of all peoples, especially through its 1948 adoption of "The Universal Declaration of Human Rights," and through its conventions called to oppose genocide and forced labor and to advocate the political rights of women.[13]

No nation is so isolated that its actions do not affect the welfare of other nations or that it is not affected by the actions of other peoples. Very perceptively Ricoeur says that ". . . today the foreign policy of every country has become the domestic policy of humanity."[14] No nation can do whatever it chooses without touching the concerns of other nations. The United Nations, with all its defects and limitations, recognizes the existence of a community of nations and attempts to bring them into effective communication with each other. Its goal is the collective confrontation of the problems of the world. Foremost among these problems is the threat of war. The UN not only proclaims the cause of peace but also sends peacekeeping forces to promote the reduction or elimination of hostilities.

Besides peacekeeping efforts the UN encourages and coordinates programs of technical assistance. "Today the spirit of the missionary motivates thousands of men and women from over half the member states of the United Nations, who go into other countries on programs of economic and cultural development."[15]

In 1973 Robert Muller, Director and Deputy to the Under-Secretary-General of the United Nations for Inter-Agency Affairs and Coordination, addressed a meeting of the American Association of Systems Analysts. He listed in impressive order the many UN agencies and programs that are dealing with the common problems of humankind—from the relationship between the planet earth and the sun to atomic energy and the preservation of the species. Muller reflects:

> It was now very clear to me: there was a pattern in all this, it was a response to a prodigious evolutionary march by the human species towards total consciousness, an attempt by man to become the all-understanding, all-enlightened, all-embracing master of his planet and of his being. Something gigantic was going on, a real turning point in evolution, the beginning of an entirely

new era of which international co-operation at the UN was only a first outward reflection.[16]

As an organization the UN specifically attempts to move beyond the narrow confines of the state and to address global issues. It is the kind of movement toward unity that should receive the encouragement and support of Christian preaching. Ricoeur states that spiritual power consists in this:

> to preserve the aim of humanity, to denounce courageously the obstacles to the unity of the human species, to expose publicly the interplay of distortions, to attack the good conscience of the wealthy, to denounce nationalism and the cult of the State, and consequently to take a stand with the greatest clarity on the limitation of sovereignty, and to show in the international institutions centered around the UN the only chance presently offered to men to move on beyond the state of the nations.[17]

Pope John Paul II acknowledged the value of the UN by addressing its assembly (October 2, 1979) and making this statement: "It [the UN] unites and associates; it does not divide and oppose. It seeks out the ways for understanding and peaceful collaboration, and endeavors with the means at its disposal and the methods in its power to exclude war, division and mutual destruction within the great family of humanity today."[18]

There are other international groups that acknowledge a world community. The International Red Cross works across national boundaries to assist people in need. The Geneva convention on issues of war outlaws certain types of warfare and advocates the proper treatment of war prisoners. Amnesty International is concerned about the status of political leaders and prisoners in all nations.

Some authors recommend an international legal system, one that would be appropriated and sanctioned by every nation of the world. The legal order would cut across state borders and would be effective especially in matters of economics and in political disputes. It would provide a peaceful and legal solution to conflicts in place of an appeal to the power of troops and instruments of war.[19]

Vatican II is not unconcerned about these global issues. It admonishes Christians to aid the needy people of the world: "Christians should willingly and wholeheartedly support the establishment of an international order that includes a genuine respect for legitimate freedom and friendly sentiments of brotherhood towards all men."[20]

Some authors speak of a federated world government, one that would bring together the various governments of the world somewhat on the order of the United States of America. The federated government would allow for legitimate regional control and legislate for matters that are truly of world-wide concern.

While not mentioning a federated government the Roman Catholic bishops of the United States advocate a political authority that encompasses the whole world. In their pastoral letter "The Challenge of Peace: God's Promise and Our Response," the bishops note: "An important element missing from world order today is a properly constituted political authority with the capacity to shape our material interdependence in the direction of moral interdependence."[21]

Some authors point up the need for diversity if a culture is to progress, if it is to be challenged to introduce new forms. T. S. Eliot reflects on cultural diversity and unity in these words: ". . . a people should be neither too united nor too divided, if its culture is to flourish. Excess of unity may be due to barbarism and may lead to tyranny; excess of division may be due to decadence and may also lead to tyranny: either excess will prevent further development in culture."[22] This principle of diversity in unity should prevail in the worldwide community of peoples. Speaking about national cultures Eliot continues: "For a national culture, if it is to flourish, should be a constellation of cultures, the constituents of which, benefiting each other, benefit the whole."[23] Eliot can even ponder the existence of a world culture which turns out to be an ideal beyond imagination: "We are therefore pressed to maintain the ideal of a world culture, while admitting that it is something we cannot *imagine*."[24]

On the religious scene there is the World Council of Churches. This is not a superchurch, not even a super Christian Church. But it is an effort to bring together Christians of different traditions and provide them with the opportunity to face together issues that confront the Christian Churches: the question of Church and society, the mission of the Church in the modern world, the Church and peace movements, the Church and economic assistance to peoples, the Church and culture. The WCC recognizes the regional traditions of Churches and the autonomy of particular traditions, but it invites them to look beyond their particular preoccupations and consider the great issues that confront their Christian brothers and sisters the world over and the issues that the Christian Church must deal with in all nations. In particular the WCC promotes an attitude of acceptance and understanding of diverse cultures. It advocates freedom from haughtiness in matters of culture. "He [Christ] offers us liberation from attitudes of cultural superiority and from self-sufficiency. He unites us in a community which transcends any particular culture."[25]

These examples should suffice to indicate that there are many movements afoot today (as there have been for centuries) toward a world community. They reveal a consistent advance toward the union of all peoples, or at least toward an appreciation of all peoples. They indicate that the groupings of people are moving closer to each other in matters of politics, law, culture, and religion. They need not be viewed as ways of suppressing regional cultures and civilizations, or national traditions and customs. The world community can exist in conjunction with regional differences.

There can be a unity of peoples on a worldwide scale and diversity of nations on a regional basis. The development of local culture is not pursued without an eye to the world community. The fathers of Vatican II noted this relationship between the development of local culture and the unification of the world: "All over the world the sense of autonomy and responsibility increases with effects of the greatest importance for the spiritual and moral maturity of mankind. This will become clearer to us if we place before our eyes the unification of the world and the duty imposed on us to build up a better world in truth and justice."[26] Again, the fathers encouraged patriotism "but without narrow-mindedness, so that they will always keep in mind the welfare of the whole human family which is formed into one by various kinds of links between races, peoples, and nations."[27]

How does theology view these movements? Does it view them as threats to the local practice of religion? Does it view them as substitutes for the religious commitment? It must be acknowledged that some people may commit themselves to these unifying movements as ultimates in their lives, as the very goal of their existence, as the end-all of human striving. Such a commitment does not disqualify the movements as such; it only calls into question the way in which the movements are evaluated. In the language of Paul Tillich such commitments are regarded as ultimates when in actuality they are not; consequently, they become idolatrous: they are not focused on the true ultimate.

Christian theology can find much good in these movements. They are concerned about peace, about sufficient levels of education for peoples, about amicable race relations, etc. The movements deal with issues that the gospel itself proclaims, for the gospel, too, is concerned about peace, union, forgiveness, assistance to the poor and the oppressed.[28] The gospel, too, has a word for the whole world. If God's concern is directed to all peoples, if the gospel and its principles are oriented to all of humankind, one can suppose that the very Spirit of God is present to all peoples to assist them in the struggle for unity and peace.

Vatican II sees values in modern scientific and technological progress:

Among these values we would like to draw attention to the following: study of the sciences and exact fidelity to truth in scientific investigation, the necessity of teamwork in technology, the sense of international solidarity, a growing awareness of the expert's responsibility to help and defend his fellow men, and an eagerness to improve the standard of living of all men, especially of those who are deprived of responsibility or suffer from cultural destitution. All these can afford a certain kind of preparation for the acceptance of the message of the Gospel and can be infused with divine charity by him who came to save the world.[29]

Walter Fishbaugh says:

If God's business is the unification of all things, then we may with reason give ourselves passionately to those enterprises in life which salute that goal and

tend, however feebly, in that direction—knowing that we go with God. No
matter how statistically intimidating the odds may be, we may set ourselves
to reconciliation and peace-making and healing and loving because we
strongly suspect that there is in this sort of endeavor a sublime logic that
goes with the grain of God's universal purposes. That ultimately we shall
fail only if God fails.[30]

It is an axiom of theology that God's gracious favor is directed to all persons and that this favor is translated into real movements of forgiveness
and peace.

God is not far from those who seek peace and work for justice. He is
not absent from those who desire to have people appreciate each other,
who wish to bring people together in harmony and concord. Theology
affirms, therefore, that movements toward a worldwide community are
themselves indications of the mind of God, are themselves patterns of
God's actions in the world. God is, after all, seeking one people, one
family.

4. Fellowship in Christ

If sin is disunity, grace is fellowship in Christ. The condition of fellowship in Christ is opposed to the condition of sin as disunity. Disunity
is inversely symbolized and effectively overcome by the kind of community that is fellowship in Jesus Christ. In the two previous sections of
this chapter, I noted the worldwide community of goods and the whole
community of humankind. Here I wish to focus specifically on the community of the Church, a fellowship of believers in Christ. The Church
of Christ is not identical with the community of all peoples; it is restricted
to those who believe in Jesus as Lord and Savior. But it is a community
that is open to the whole of humankind and in fact is found in most peoples
of the world.

The Church is a place where isolation is superseded by a person's
fellowship with Jesus Christ and with those who believe in his lordship:
"If we say, 'We have fellowship with him,' while continuing to walk in
darkness, we are liars and do not act in truth. But if we walk in light, as he
is in the light, we have fellowship with one another, and the blood of his
Son Jesus cleanses us from all sin" (1 John 1:6). The word "fellowship"
translates the Greek *koinonia*, a term which denotes participation. *Koinonia* refers primarily to the intimate bond of sharing that is established
by participation in a reality. "Paul uses *κοινωνία* for the religious fellowship (participation) of the believer in Christ and Christian blessings, and
for the mutual fellowship of believers."[31] Fellowship in Christ means
spiritual communion with Christ, a sharing in the risen life that indeed
commences now but will be perfected in a time to come. It is a fellowship
which begins with God the Father in the sense that he calls people to fellowship with his Son: "God is faithful, and it was he who called you to

fellowship with his Son, Jesus Christ our Lord" (1 Cor 1:9). He will also crown this fellowship in some future event, but always with and in Jesus Christ.

Fellowship with Christ implies a union with him in the various phases of his life: witness to the word of the Father, suffering, death, and resurrection. Just as the original disciples of Jesus shared his company, his word, his passion, death and resurrection, so also his disciples today share his word, his sufferings, and his risen life. The distance in time between the initial life of Christ and his presence today does not constitute an obstacle; for Jesus is living and active today, and he continues a vital relationship with his followers. Fellowship with Christ also implies sharing in his Spirit: "The grace of the Lord Jesus Christ, and the love of God, and the fellowship of the Holy Spirit be with you all!" (2 Cor 13:13) The Spirit is a power in the community, and Paul prays that the believers may share in his powerful presence and gracious gifts.

An individual's fellowship with Christ entails a fellowship with all who believe in Christ, with all who share his life. Christian fellowship means union in Christ. Christ is the central figure toward whom individual believers are oriented, but since individuals are directed to Christ as to their focal point, they are also related to each other in Christ. Christ becomes the major aspect of their relationship to each other. There are many other aspects, to be sure, such as life in common on this planet, common speech, etc. But the most significant dimension of their relationship is the personal life of Jesus Christ. The primary importance of Christ follows from his very Sonship, his Incarnational manifestation of the very life of God. He can be no other than the turning point of the new age of the world.

Fellowship with other believers implies service and assistance. The mutual assistance took very tangible form for Saint Paul when he promoted and secured a collection from the missionary churches outside Palestine to help the poor Jewish Christians in Jerusalem.

> Just now I am leaving for Jerusalem to bring assistance to the saints. Macedonia and Achaia have kindly decided to make a contribution for those in need among the saints in Jerusalem. They did so of their own accord, yet they are also under obligation. For if the Gentiles have shared in the spiritual blessings of the Jews, they ought to contribute to their temporal needs in return (Rom 15:25-27; cf. 1 Cor 16:1-4; 2 Cor 8:1—9:15).

Saint Paul lists a number of reasons for helping the poor of Jerusalem. The Jewish Christians of Jerusalem were economically poor. Therefore, charity was a motive. Moreover, since the Jewish Christians shared the blessings of the faith with the Gentiles, it was fitting for the Gentiles to assist them in return. Paul was especially concerned about the unity of Jewish and Gentile Christians in the one fellowship of Christ; the collection was an effective symbol of this oneness.

In brief, by organizing the collection and insisting that participation in it be a volitionary act of Christian love expressing the reciprocal concern inherent to the Christian fellowship, Paul relied on it to testify to the Jerusalem Christians of the real and full inclusion of Gentile believers into the Body of Christ. He further trusted that this testimony would be so unequivocal that they would be moved to restore complete and unconditional bonds of fellowship with the Gentiles.[32]

Shared life in Christ is not a mental manipulation of concepts. It is an experienced life in Christ, an experiential knowledge of one's union in Christ. It is the kind of sharing that reaches all levels of one's existence —understanding, feeling, loving, enjoying, sorrowing. It is shared Christian existence that reaches all levels of knowing and choosing, touching and tasting, hearing and speaking. Life in fellowship with Christ is not confined to the imperceptible, though certainly the transcendent character of Jesus is not subject to minute empirical analysis. Fellowship with Christ is a shared life in the truth and goodness of the Father that is manifest in Christ.

Fellowship in Christ is a community of belief. It is a union of those who share a common commitment to the person and word of Jesus. To believe in Christ is to share in the common belief of others. This does not mean that every Christian believer has precisely the same impression of the person of Jesus or has the same degree of commitment to him. Christians differ from each other in their measure of faith—both as a gift and as a commitment. But the range of unity of those who believe in the lordship of Jesus far outreaches the elements of difference. There is a broad sharing in the one faith which was summed up by Paul in the confession "Jesus is Lord" (1 Cor 12:3) and which is crystallized by the many creeds that were composed by the Church through the ages. There is a community of faith, existing as a force that overcomes isolation and disunity. The community of faith is opposed to the disunity of sin.

Fellowship in Christ implies a sharing of hope. The word of Christ supplies hope for the human community, an outcome to the many puzzlements and anxieties of human existence. Christian believers share a common hope in the person of Jesus; they look to him as the source of confidence that their sins are forgiven, that there is union with God, that there is some meaning to human life. Fellowship in Christ supplies mutual hope in the sense that believers assist each other in searching the roots of hope, in announcing the foundation of hope, and in proclaiming the direction of hope. The word of hope in the fellowship of believers is an important aspect of community. A fellowship of hope overcomes the sin of disunity and the fatalism of despair.

Fellowship in Christ also implies a sharing in love. Christ is the very Incarnation of the love of God for humankind. Those who are united to him by faith and love are themselves the manifestation of the love of God.

Their sharing in the love of Christ and in his manifestation of the love of God makes them a community of love—a community of concern, affection, understanding, and forgiveness.[33] Love is the greatest gift of God. This becomes available to those who believe in Christ; it is available to the whole of humankind but centrally focused in a special way in the community of Christian believers. Fellowship in Christ is formed by the love of God in Christ, and the love-formed community itself fosters love in the human community. Fellowship in love exists as a mode of overcoming the fellowship of hate. The fellowship of Christian love provides a way of overcoming the isolation and loneliness of disunity. The fellowship of love is itself a grace, a gift that opposes the forces of division.

It is by being loved in community (the family, the neighborhood, the Church) that one learns to love in return. "It is only by a return of love that the communion comes about, the perfect community of persons in which the lovers are completely themselves and at home in one another."[34] God's initial love creates a community of appreciative love. Being loved by God and others provides the very power of love. Love is the ever intensifying feedback of power within the community. It is the Christian hope that the multitude of communities of love will join in a worldwide fellowship of love: "He [the Word of God] assures those who trust in the charity of God that the way of love is open to all men and that the effort to establish a universal brotherhood will not be in vain."[35]

Christian fellowship is the place where sinners are aided in their search for re-union with God. In the Christian community sinners experience the presence of God through a group of believers who are accepting and caring. The Christian fellowship exists to manifest the presence of God. "The prisoner, the sick person, the Christian in exile sees in the companionship of a fellow Christian a physical sign of the gracious presence of the triune God. Visitor and visited in loneliness recognize in each other the Christ who is present in the body; they receive and meet each other as one meets the Lord, in reverence, humility, and joy."[36] This is not to say that the Lord is not encountered elsewhere in the world nor that the community is a perfect image of the Lord. But it is to say that the perceptible community is a full and living sign of the Lord's presence, and as such it is the place where persons of sin and disunity can effectively meet the Lord and enjoy the fruits of communion, both with the Lord and with the members of his body.

The Lord is encountered in the midst of Christian fellowship because the gathering is his body. He is encountered because the Christian fellowship announces his word and celebrates his sacraments. The Lord is present in his word; he makes it communicative and effective in the mouths of those who proclaim it. "But God has put this Word into the mouth of men in order that it may be communicated to other men. When one person is struck by the Word, he speaks it to others."[37] Those who are united in Christ speak his word and his word is itself a rallying point, a center of unity which draws together those who allow themselves to receive the word, those who find themselves distracted and pulled apart. The word moves people from disunity to community.

Fellowship in Christ implies a community of worship. Christian believers do not pray in isolation from the others who share their commitment to the person of Jesus. They may, indeed must, pray privately, to be sure; but prayer always has a communal dimension; it is offered for others in the community, it is offered with their support, it is offered in union with them. Christian believers must also pray publicly. Community worship, especially in celebration of the Eucharist, is the high point of Christian existence. At worship the Christian fellowship is manifest as the community of God in Christ Jesus. "Is not the cup of blessing we bless a sharing in the blood of Christ? And is not the bread we break a sharing in the body of Christ?" (1 Cor 10:16) The community is visibly gathered to proclaim the name of God, to laud his benefits, to petition his grace. Worship brings the fellowship of Christians together and at the same time draws them close with the tight bonds of word and sacrament. Worship is the place where disunity is overcome, where harmful divisions are laid aside for the sake of a common approach to the throne of the Father. The fellowship of worship both invites the isolated to join in a common praise of God and fosters union of those who are assembled together. The community of worship reaches beyond the disunity of prayerless aloofness.

The fellowship in Christ fosters a respect for life: for human life and all life on this planet. It fosters a respect for the goods of the earth. When persons are brought into fellowship with Christ and his community, they are led to absorb the concept of the goodness of all creation (cf. Genesis 1 and Psalm 8) and the value of human life. This is not to say, of course, that the Christian fellowship is necessarily outstanding in these areas of respect, nor that no respect is found elsewhere. It only means that the main tradition of the fellowship is respect for the goodness of the earth and for the value of human existence. Christian fellowship means communion with the material of the planet and with the flesh of humankind, which Jesus himself did not reject. Fellowship means sharing with others in a very concrete way the energies and shapes of this earth. If the sin of disunity can arise because of alienation from the earth or positive disdain for the forces of the earth, the Christian fellowship is there to teach a reciprocity between human life and the planet and a loving respect for the forces of the earth. Disunity, the division between self and the world, is overcome at least initially through the mutual sharing of the goods of the earth, its elements that are caught up in the sacraments (bread, water, oil), its food that is needed for nourishment, its buildings that are needed for shelter, its land that is needed for a sense of place and home. The willfully directed respect for the world is a movement toward the reconciliation of the voluntary and the involuntary, the willful and the nonwillful, the tractable and the resistant.

Fellowship in Christ means mutual forgiveness. Fellowship means that everyone comes to the community from a position of sin.[38] In fact, everyone brings sin to the fellowship and seeks there an understanding of the dimensions of failure. He or she does not expect the fellowship to approve of the sin but to note it for the disruption that it is and help the self to move beyond it to community.[39] Humans do not bring about reconciliation by their own power. God the Father is the source of reconciliation, and Christ is the agent. "All this has been done by God, who has reconciled us to himself through Christ and has given us the ministry of reconciliation" (2 Cor 5:18). God's activity in Christ effects reconciliation, but Christians carry on the work of Christ in proclamation and forgiveness. The reconciling work of God has consequences for the human community. It breaks down the enmity between Jews and Gentiles and draws humans together in community. "It is he [Christ] who is our peace, and who made the two of us one by breaking down the barriers of hostility that kept us apart" (Eph 2:14). The Christian fellowship is there to gather the sinner to itself, to proclaim the forgiving word of God, and to lead the sinner to union with God and with itself. The two unions are not entirely distinct. It is precisely through union with the fellowship that union with God is repaired. Christian fellowship is the mode of reconciliation between the human sinner and the divine presence.

Realistic entry into community is the access to fellowship with the Father, the Son, and their mutual Spirit. Fellowship brings about an association with the accepting love of God in Christ. It means that the sinner moves away from the condition of hostility and estrangement and is restored to peaceful relationship with God. "For if, when we were God's enemies, we were reconciled to him by the death of his Son, it is all the more certain that we who have been reconciled will be saved by his life. Not only that; we go so far as to make God our boast through our Lord Jesus Christ, through whom we have now received reconciliation" (Rom 5:10-11). Harold Ditmanson sums up the notion of reconciliation as grace in these words: "But if we hold in combination the overcoming of estrangement and hostility, the specific association with the love of God or of Christ, the full restoration of relationship, and the stress of rejoicing, then we have in reconciliation an image of peculiar intensity and of great positive force."[40] Reconciliation is a traditional word, especially in Protestant theology, referring to the overcoming of the situation of sin and hostility. The term reveals well the bringing together of two estranged parties, God and humankind.

The fellowship in Christ becomes a community of salvation, the place where there is forgiveness of sin, healing of spirits, and reconciliation with the Father. ". . . healing means reuniting that which is estranged, giving a center to what is split, overcoming the split between God and man, man and his world, man and himself."[41] Salvation is healing, making whole, bringing together, rendering sound. It is a healing, not only for the self, but also for the community; not for just a small group of elite, but for a huge community. "Because God is so boundlessly gracious, because God loves sinners, Jesus does not gather the holy remnant, but the all-embracing community of salvation of God's new people."[42] It is not a small community of salvation that God gathers; it is the large community of Christian believers that are rejoicing in the favor of God's forgiveness. Saint Paul sees the community as a union of Jews and Gentiles: "It is he [Christ] who is our peace, and who made the two of us one by breaking down the barrier of hostility that kept us apart" (Eph 2:14). But forgiveness and peace are not confined to explicit fellowship in Christ. It is a teaching of Vatican II, one that has its roots in the Scriptures themselves,[43] that people may find forgiveness and union with God outside the boundaries of the Christian religion. "Wherever man transcends himself in unselfish love and invests in genuine liberating efforts with others, there Christ is present, even if those involved are not conscious of it. Whenever man refuses the solidarity in salvation he is, of necessity, opting for solidarity in corruption and implicitly rejects Christ."[44] The principle of forgiveness is still the saving life and death of Jesus, but there is a lack of recognition of this principle for reasons that vary from the absence of an evangelist to the unconvincing announcement of the gospel message and the poor example of Christian believers. Even when forgiveness is achieved outside explicit Christianity, the persons so reconciled are not without forms of community and they are not without an orientation toward others in their society. The forgiveness can be manifest, can become incarnated in various ways, such as a search for peace and justice in their society, a concern for the poor and the oppressed, a love for truth, a respect for family and civic communities. Without describing this situation in detail—for it is beyond the scope of this study—it must be noted that reconciliation and forgiveness, wherever they are accomplished, have a communitarian dimension, lead to fellowship and community, or at least strengthen the existing bonds of authentic community.

The community is a place of freedom. It is a place where humans find release from the bonds of isolation. Community is "a being-free from the bond of our own self, a liberation from the solitariness and the limitations in which self-love detains us."[45] Community provides a person with the power to move from a destructive isolation to an other-directed, loving relation to others. Without community there is exclusivity and aloneness. With community there is the possibility of moving out to others in care and love. Such a movement is not only of benefit to the community by reason of the loving deeds that the person does to build up the community, but it is also of benefit to the individual involved in the movement, for it allows him or her to become free from selfish isolation and to develop talents of love and understanding. Freedom can be "strengthened by accepting the inevitable constraints of social life, by understanding the manifold demands of human fellowship, and by service to the community at large."[46]

It is true that no one can survive without the attending care of some community (family, association, village, etc.); it is also true that communities vary considerably in their ability to foster freedom. Some families provide a milieu, not of total license, but of cautious restraint, where the limits and possibilities of freedom can be tested. Some nations provide an extraordinary range of civic freedoms for their citizens, others an extremely limited one. The community of the church provides a milieu of freedom from the debilitating isolation of sin and relate the sinner both to God and to other believers. The forgiving presence of God can be symbolized and effected by many other communities that are not explicitly religious. Whatever group provides and fosters true freedom expresses the truth and will of God.

Fellowship brings a milieu of love, an exchange of truth, an evidence of compassion, and a test of honesty. Christian fellowship is thus the place where hate, dishonesty, and disinterestedness are overcome. It is the place where the Holy Spirit resides with his gifts of truth and forgiveness. Saint Paul exhorts the Philippians to pattern their community life on the mind of Christ: "In the name of the encouragement you owe me in Christ, in the name of the solace that love can give, of fellowship in spirit, compassion, and pity, I beg you: Make my joy complete by your unanimity, possessing the one love, united in spirit and ideals" (Phil 2:1-2). Christian fellowship entails a united spirit, a oneness in compassion. It is precisely this oneness in spirit that provides the sinner with the opportunity to overcome isolation and disunity and to become reconciled to God in the midst of the community.

5. The Monastic Community[47]

The community of the Church is an effective symbol of grace and union. The monastic community that abides in the midst of the Church may be regarded as paradigmatic of the grace of community. The monastery can symbolize many, but not all, of the features of grace that accrue to the reality of community. Just as the church brings to focus the multivalent dimensions of the human community at large, so also the monastic community brings to focus the communitarian dimensions of the Church.[48]

The monastery as a community has the features of a local Church. It is an *ecclesiola*, a small gathering of Christian people who believe in the lordship of Jesus Christ and who desire to lead a life in accordance with this belief. The monastery as Church is governed by the words of the gospel and by the tradition of the Church through the ages. The monks of the monastic community are dedicated to prayer, the search for God, service, hope, and expectation. They are guided by the Scriptures and the tradition of the Church, governed by superiors, dedicated to the liturgy of prayer and sacraments, and concerned about a mission to the wider Church and to the civic community. In short, the monastery as Church is a miniature symbol of the multidimensional features of the universal Church.

The monastery is modeled on the idealized Church of Jerusalem as pictured in the summary statements of the Acts of the Apostles. Saint Luke characterizes the primitive Church as a gathering of believers in Jesus Christ, as a community dedicated to the apostles' teaching, to prayer, and to a sharing of goods:

> They devoted themselves to the apostles' instruction and the communal life, to the breaking of bread and the prayers. . . . Those who believed shared all things in common; they would sell their property and goods, dividing everything on the basis of each one's need. They went to the temple area together every day, while in their homes they broke bread. With exultant and sincere hearts they took their meals in common, praising God and winning the approval of all the people" (Acts 2:42, 44-47a; cf. 4:32-37; 5:12-16).

The primitive community of Jerusalem is the acknowledged model of cenobitic monasticism.

The monastery can function as a paradigm of the Church and of the human community because it is a visible, identifiable group of people within the wider community of the Church and society. The monastic community is located in a place, rooted in the land of a particular environment, and situated in a definite culture. While the monastery is to some extent removed from the culture of the place, it is also marked by the cultural patterns of a specific society. It speaks its language; it abides generally by its economic structures; it is related to the families of a region.

In one sense, the monastic community lives on the margin of the Church and of society; in another sense, it is in the center. The monastery certainly is not large, and for many people it can remain unnoticed. But its marginal character can also be its strength. Precisely because it does not blend entirely into the local culture, it can function as a symbol of community and a symbol of grace. It can portray symbolically the desired or ideal features of community: unity, goal-directedness, mutual service, leadership, hope, tradition, instruction. The monastery can function as a prophetic community that provides a symbolic word and practice for society at large. It is marginal in the sense that it is not in the mainstream of societal patterns, but it is central in the sense that it represents significant features of any valid community.

The monastery is a stable gathering of Christians, even though individual monks may enter or leave the local congregation for reasons of work, recreation, business, or professional advancement. The monastery is an ongoing, visible, identifiable gathering of Christian believers who bring to expression the on-going, visible, and identifiable characteristics of the Church at large.

Monks are a local gathering of disciples of Christ; they are united with each other because they are joined to Christ. Their bonds of communion are precisely the life of Christ and the love of God. It is because the monks are instructed with faith in God and in his Son Jesus Christ that they agree to live together in community and to pursue a life of prayer and service. Because of their common dedication to the ideals of the gospel and the search for God, they experience a communion with one another.

The horizontal relationships within the monastic community are founded on the many doctrinal and liturgical bonds that characterize the Church as a whole. Monks gather together in the name of Christ and in the power of the Holy Spirit. The divine power at work in them does not confine their life to a vertical relationship to God. To be sure, the transcendent relation to God remains primary for every monk, but it does not exclude the horizontal relationship of monk to monk. Saint Benedict's favorite term for this horizontal relationship is *congregatio*, "flock" or "gathering." The monastic community is like a gathering of sheep with Christ as the supreme pastor. The monks gather in one flock under one Shepherd.

Frater (brother) is another word that Benedict uses to denote the horizontal relationship between members of the monastic community. The word "brother" is the traditional term for associates of the Christian faith, even in the New Testament. Monastic legislators use the term to characterize the believers who constitute the members of a monastery, so closely joined one to another that they can be compared to the brothers of the primitive Church. The term "brother," of course, stems from the family context, but its primary reference in monastic usage is the Church of the New Testament. The members of the monastery are brothers because they are united in Christian faith and love.

The *Rule of Benedict* uses the word *frater* dozens of times, but *fraternitas* ("brotherhood") only once, in Chapter 72, "The Good Zeal of Monks."[49] Saint Benedict urges monks to be respectful of one another, to manifest mutual obedience, and to love each other: "To their fellow monks they show the pure love of brothers" (RB 72:8). The horizontal relationship is manifested in obedience and love, but it culminates in the love for Christ, for Benedict wants his monks to prefer nothing to Christ (RB 72:11).

The members of the brotherhood are responsible not just to the abbot and the other officials of the monastery but also to one another. They are mutually responsible for the work of liturgical prayer, for the maintenance and support of the monastery, for the spirit of obedience and encouragement. They offer their advice to the whole community in matters that pertain to the whole brotherhood. They share collegially in the governance of the goods of the monastery, always under the primary stewardship of the abbot and under the general regulations of ecclesiastical law.

The monastery is a gathering of those who are in "a school for the Lord's service" (RB Prologue 45). A school, in the original sense of the term, is an assembly of soldiers, workers, or students; it is also the name of the place in which these groups assemble. The monastery as a school is the place for the gathering of monks; it is the assembly of those who have the leisure to devote themselves to the study of the divine word and to the service of Christ. Christ, in fact, is the Teacher in the school: "Take my yoke upon you, and learn from me; for I am gentle and lowly of heart" (Matt 11:29). Just as the Church is a place of salvific instruction, so also is the monastery a place of education in the wisdom of God. The monks learn to read and to study the Scriptures. Through the centuries the monks not only taught their own brothers how to read and to write but also developed schools of learning for others.

The school of the Lord's service, therefore, includes instruction in divine wisdom, but it also develops cultural wisdom of all sorts. As such, the monastery is a community where there is respect for the arts of reading and writing, music and painting. The school of the monastery is not remote from the modern arts of architecture, painting, film, poetry, etc. It is acquainted with these arts and is able to dialogue with those who pursue them elsewhere; the monastery contributes its own wisdom that stems from a long tradition of respect and love for arts and crafts.

The monastic community may function as a symbol of service. There is first of all the mutual service which the brothers render to one another. There is service in the kitchen and at table; the service of teaching; the service of pursuing crafts for the benefit of the monks and for the financial support of the monastery; service at the altar, the ministry of word and sacrament; the service of mutual encouragement and counseling; service of the sick. The *Rule of Benedict* urges special care of the sick because it is especially in them that Christ is served: "Care of the sick must rank above and before all else, that they may truly be served as Christ" (RB 36:1).

Monastic tradition generally and the *Rule of Benedict* in particular command the care of guests and pilgrims: "All guests who present themselves are to be welcomed as Christ, for he himself will say: 'I was a stranger and you welcomed me'" (RB 53:1; Mt 25:35). The monastery can provide a great service to fellow Christians and also to others by offering them a place apart for reflection, rest, and prayer. Married couples, groups of students, or individuals can find the quiet of the monastery a welcome respite from their daily activities, and they can find encouragement in their faith by joining the monks at prayer or by discussing matters of concern with them. The instruction is mutual: the monks benefit from the presence of fellow believers, from their experience, and from their insights into the human condition; the guests in turn are assisted by the regular life, prayer, readings and conversations shared with the monks.

The monastery as a community is not an aggregate of monks without head or direction. It has a leadership structure that is designed for the maximum good of the individual monk and is modeled on that of Jesus and his disciples. In fact, the abbot, the father of the monastery, represents Christ to the monks and is related to the monks as Jesus was to his disciples. "He is believed to hold the place of Christ in the monastery, since he is addressed by a title of Christ" (RB 2:2). As Christ's leadership of his disciples was one of instruction and direction, so also the abbot's leadership of the monks is one of teaching and direction. The abbot teaches and governs, not for the sake of some personal goal such as self-esteem or self-aggrandizement, but for the sake of the monks. His leadership is exercised in service to others.

The abbot, as spiritual father to the whole community, carefully discerns what is correct and proper for each of the monks. He is a healer of wounded spirits, pouring in the balm of the divine Scriptures and his own studied wisdom. He is the shepherd who guides his flock to green pastures and healthy nourishment.

The abbot of the monastic community is not to govern in an autocratic manner but is to seek counsel from the whole monastery. He is obliged to receive the approval of the community in financial matters and in concerns that pertain to the urgent well-being of the monastery, e.g., recruitment, educational enterprises, etc. Ideally he will seek to achieve a consensus of the community in the matters that he brings up for consideration. In any event, his position of leadership is not such that it precludes the sharing of responsibility with the members of the community. Concerned leadership that shares responsibility is a model of leadership for many human communities.

The abbot's leadership is not designed to crush the responsibility of the individual monk. Monastic obedience is not structured in such a way that only the abbot is responsible for his commands; the monk is also responsible for the commands that he follows. In other words, the individual monk cannot assume a stance of uncritical obedience. The object of abbatial leadership is not to brainwash or to control minds. It is not the kind of obedience demanded by the Reverend Jim Jones who commanded his followers to commit suicide.[50] The abbot-disciple relationship is one of maximum benefit for the individual monk. The disciple listens and obeys because he esteems the wise direction and the discernment of the abbot. The abbot's leadership is exercised for the spiritual profit of the disciple, not for domination over him.

Finally, the community finds an important dimension of unity in the person of the abbot. His figure stands as a point of focus for the whole community, its center of vision and direction, its animating support, and its spokesman for the monastic tradition.

The monastic community receives guidance from the abbot, who embodies within himself the wisdom of tradition. The abbot is a norm of living, both in what he says and in what he does. He himself, of course, is not without direction in his abbatial office. The gospels and church leadership provide him with a ready pattern of speaking and acting; so also do the lives of the monastic fathers and the rules of conduct which they established for monastic living. There is especially the *Rule of Benedict*, which provides much wisdom that is still applicable today; the centrality of seeking God and of prayer; concern for the individual; the importance of reading the scriptures, etc. Many details of the Rule are no longer feasible or commendable, but even these indicate a pattern of how the monastic spirit must be embodied in concrete guidelines.

The abbot, therefore, is not free to direct a monastic community according to his own whim and fancy. He himself must be governed by the Scriptures, by monastic tradition, by the *Rule of Benedict*, by the good norms of human psychology and counseling, by the needs of the present time. His monks can expect a certain protection under the Rule and under the guidelines of tradition. They can expect a certain pattern of living which will allow them to pursue the goals of monastic life: the seeking of God, prayer, and service. They can expect a certain freedom under the Rule, that is, they can expect that their ability to choose and to be responsible will not be diminished under the Rule and the abbot, but that their life will be supported and graced in its search for God and for service of others. The monks can expect a certain degree of equality under the Rule; they can expect that the abbot will not show favoritism but that he will relate to each and share with each as equitably as possible. This does not mean, of course, that everyone receives the same opportunities and benefits. Talents differ from person to person; so also do needs. In short, the monastic community offers an example of leadership that is itself governed by a tradition and that provides for the maximum freedom and well-being of individuals.

The monastic community is also a place of personal development. The monastic life does not promise the fulfillment of self only in the end, in some future world. At the present time and in the midst of the community there is the possibility of self-development and self-understanding, of growth in grace and understanding. Through contact with others in work and prayer, in recreation and dialogue, in discourse and counsel, the individual monk learns about self and is taught the vision of the Christian life. In listening to others in the monastery, especially to the abbot, the official teacher of the community, the monk learns to measure self against the norms of Christian and monastic living and to discern the way in which God is leading him. He also learns about his strengths and weaknesses.

There is place for emotional exchange in the monastery; there is place for encouragement and support. There is place for the mutual sharing of gifts and charisms, which are given not for personal aggrandizement, but for the building up of the community. Through the development of these gifts the whole community is built up into a witness to the Transcendent and into a place of service.

The monastery is also a place to learn mutual obedience, love, and patience. It is not a place where everyone is alike. The personality of each monk is different from that of the next. Characteristic shortcomings and defects are present in each monk. Benedict realizes the patience that monks need to exercise toward each other; therefore, he urges patience and forebearance: "They should try to be the first to show respect to the other, supporting with greatest patience one another's weaknesses of body or behavior, and earnestly competing in obedience to one another" (RB 72:4-6).

Cenobitic monasticism differs from eremitical monasticism precisely in this: the monks do not live alone; they have the daily opportunity to bear with one another patiently, to obey each other, and to offer fraternal correction. "He who dwells with brethren must not be square, but round, so as to turn himself towards all," the desert father Matoes says.[51] Cenobitic monks find self-development by constantly turning to others in forebearance and service.

Cenobitic monasticism can function as a paradigm of grace, but it also contains within itself a dimension of sin. Individual monks themselves have not achieved the perfection of love and service; they are pilgrims on the way to full enjoyment of God. They find in themselves selfishness and self will, envy and anger, laziness and pride. They are in continual need of admonition that comes from the sacred scriptures, from the lips of the abbot, and from one another.

There is also the danger of community egoism. The whole monastic community can focus its attention only on itself. It can turn into a community that only knows how to admire itself, that only knows how to serve itself. Instead of looking out beyond its own boundaries to the service of the whole church, the monastic community can be attentive only to its own interests. This does not mean that every cenobitic monastery must assume some outside work, but it does mean that the community can serve others through witness, writing, caring for guests, and teaching. Community egoism can be overcome by attention to the needs of the Church and people of a region.

In summary, we can say that the monastery as a place of community and grace is an assembly in Christ, a gathering in the name of Christ. Saint Benedict calls the monastery the "house of God" (RB 31:19, 53: 22, 64:5). It is the place where his word is enthroned and proclaimed, where monks seek the presence and glory of God, where Christ is represented in the abbot, the sick, and the guests. It is the place where believers are already in communion with Christ and expect to be brought forward into the communion of eternal life: "Let them [the monks] prefer nothing whatever to Christ, and may he bring us all together to everlasting life" (RB 72:11-12). Communion in Christ is a grace, and the goal of the communion is continual life with God in Christ.

The monastery, therefore, as a group of believers, effectively symbolizes and brings about the milieu of grace and forgiveness, of hope and loving communion. As a movement within the Church, it is a model of the type of communion that Jesus offers us in the reign of God.

6. The Symbol of the City

Is the city a community? Can the city be a symbol of grace? Or is it rather a symbol of sin? Should not one turn from the city to the desert, the forest, or the rural countryside, locations that are frequently and traditionally cited as places of innocence and reflection? What is the value of the city? Is it an aberration of the human mind? Is it a failure?

From one standpoint the city can be viewed as a community; it is the gathering in a fairly restricted area of a great number of citizens. In a smaller city the people are more obviously located around a central core of commercial, industrial, and recreational establishments. In a larger city they are more likely gathered in a core area and a number of sub-centers. But even in the case of larger cities the concept of civic community prevails, although it might be more appropriate to speak of the city as an aggregate of communities.

My purpose, however, is not to argue a particular definition of city or to examine the many aspects of the urban community. My purpose is, rather, to look at the city as a form of community and as a symbol of grace. It is true that the city is often seen as a place of sin ("sin city"). There can be no doubt about the presence of sin in the city. Just as a sinful dimension characterizes any human community, so there is sin in the midst of the city. The dimension of sin is often painfully evident; no day or hour passes without the report of fraud and violent crime. The concentration of people in a small area brings to focus the dimension of sin, a fraction of which gets reported in the media. The city can symbolize sin, but it can also symbolize grace. It is the aspect of grace that I wish to consider here.

The city of Jerusalem, secured by David as his throne city, received the admiration of the people of Israel as a place of God's dwelling, as the chosen site of his presence, as a refuge of his elect. But it was also the place of intrigue and infidelity. The pre-exilic prophets lamented the loss of faith in Yahweh, and some of them predicted the destruction of the holy city. The exiles in Babylon looked back upon the city of Jerusalem and its temple with nostalgia and longed for the restoration of the land and its capital city. Jerusalem was indeed a vision of peace, but its beauty was often marred by sin and destruction.

Jesus, too, went up to the city of Jerusalem as to the place of his Father's house. He desired to gather the people of the city together in the power and truth of his message, but he was rejected. The conversation of Jesus with the Samaritan women at Jacob's well indicated that the city of Jerusalem with its temple is not the exclusive place of divine worship in spirit and truth.

The Jerusalem of the Book of Revelation appears as a heavenly city, a city of peace and salvation: ". . . the holy city Jerusalem coming down out of heaven from God. It gleamed with the splendor of God. . . . I saw no temple in the city. The Lord, God the Almighty, is its temple—he and the Lamb. The city had no need of sun or moon, for the glory of God gave it light, and its lamp was the Lamb" (21:10-11, 22-23). The city, specifically the city of Jerusalem, forms the symbol of the gathering place of the world to come, the place of the Lamb. It is a symbol of brightness and glory, the seat of God and his elect. "For here we have no lasting city: we are seeking one which is to come" (Heb 13:14).

The Greek *polis* is an already established city of order and rationality, a place of words and persuasion rather than of force and violence.[52] It provides a sense of identity for the citizen, but not for the slave who works in the city and who does not reap all its benefits. The city is governed democratically; therefore, it allows its citizens to participate in the definition of its policies. The involvement in the city is nearly total; it is a place of security and an environment of personal development. It provides a generally peaceful and harmonious life for the people. It is a city-state, a self-enclosed community where each person is never far from the center of the common life.

The biblical Jerusalem and the Greek city-state are classic symbols of cities. They symbolize the life of splendor and peace or the existence of harmony and rationality. There are other urban symbols in the history of humankind, e.g., the medieval feudal city, the Renaissance city. These are mentioned to remind us that the city is symbolic of the best in human life, even while it may contain evils and failures or even when it distributes its favors sparingly and selectively. The city is indeed a symbol of grace, a community of favor.

Without becoming rhapsodic about the glories of the city, as was the vogue in the 1960's,[53] one can identify dimensions of the civic community that reverse the trends of sin. There are features of urban existence that overcome, at least to some extent, the condition of division and disunity. The forces of unity and community are opposed to the forces of disunity.

The city provides the opportunity for personal development. It encourages the arts: music education and musical performances are at hand; art and architecture are present to enjoy and to pursue; libraries are available for preserving the best of human experience and for cultivating the human spirit; theater and film recreate and instruct the spirit; spectator sports are a daily recreational occurrence; facilities are available for exercising the human body. These opportunities are not panaceas for the divisions that one finds within oneself, disunities of mind and spirit, disharmonies of body and soul. But they are helpful in their power to heal, to make whole and wholesome, and to bring together again the split ends of the human unit.

The city also provides the opportunity for education, from pre-school to university and post-graduate study. It brings together in a relatively small space scholars from many fields and encourages their interaction. The city is the place for the human psyche to reach a high pitch of activity as it relates to the academic and civic spheres of intelligence. It encourages the person to develop self and to correct one's position by the constant criticism of others.

The city provides opportunities for employment; it brings together a cluster of industrial and business enterprises that makes it possible for persons to take pride in supporting themselves and their families. The city offers a great variety of jobs so that people of the most varying talent can find employment that suits their abilities and tastes. If the city is properly arranged—as it usually is not—the people can find work within a reasonable distance from their place of residence. At least there is the occasional possibility for people to locate near their place of employment. So many goods and services are available in the midst of the city that it is possible for persons to pursue a life of relative comfort without the fear of deprivation.

Health care is also readily available in the city. The city can bring together a concentration of health care facilities as well as a skillful group of physicians and nurses. The city can also promote educational programs of preventive medicine: the importance of proper food and diet, the value of physical exercise, the meaning of special care for the young and the elderly.

In short, the city is a place of intense cultural development. It gathers in a restricted space a great variety of people, institutions, and programs that enhance human culture. An interchange of ideas, art forms, literary expressions, etc., can stimulate a climate of intellectual and spiritual development. The rapid and intense interaction of citizens raises the psychic and spiritual pitch of the people; it results in a complexification, to use the term of Teilhard de Chardin.

The city, whether it is viewed as one community or as an aggregate of communities, symbolizes and effects the togetherness of peoples. It symbolizes and effects the grace of living in community. Living in community provides the opportunity for personal healing, for development of mind, body, and spirit, for the preservation and enhancement of culture, for interaction with others in a spirit of mutual trust and support.

There are dimensions of grace in the community of the city. This means that there are dimensions of the urban community which are God-willed and Spirit-directed. God is not absent from those who reach out and assist people who are in physical and mental pain. He is not absent from those who wish to enhance the human community by their artistic and intellectual talents. He is not absent from those who wish to govern the community for the sake of the health and well-being of all people. He is not absent from those who wish to preserve the best of the tradition, even as they extend the realm of knowledge. He is not confined to the assembly of Christian believers, even though his word and will are manifest in a special way in their midst. The Church is necessary as a place where the presence and activity of God are remembered and effected in word and sacrament. The Church has the task of proclaiming and realizing this word in the face of the world. But the assembly of Christian believers is not the only force at work in the community. There are widespread movements for up-grading the effectiveness of government, health care, instruction in schools, communication, etc., movements which do not stem directly from the work of the Church. These movements are not without gracious effect or without the favor of God. He is present beyond the borders of the Church to bring about the good of community.

When Christian believers engage in activities that bring about the well-being of the city, they are not occupied with matters that have no value in the sight of God. Christianity is concerned about the human community, the good ordering of the city. The fathers of Vatican Council II condemn the error of non-involvement: "But it is no less mistaken to think that we may immerse ourselves in earthly activities as if these latter were utterly foreign to religion, and religion were nothing more than the

fulfillment of acts of worship and the observance of a few moral obliga-
tions."[54] The council uses traditional two-city terminology to the effect
that the believer is a citizen of both cities and has responsibilities to each.[55]

Since the issue here is the grace of the urban community, it is sufficient to cite—as the inverse of grace—the many perils of the city. It does
not require much experience or attentiveness to the communication
media to realize that the city is also a place of grinding poverty for many
of its residents (think of the barrios of many cities in South America or
of the inner core of many cities of the United States). It is a place of violence and crime; death and assault stalk many of the city's streets. It is
a place of neglect as many powerless people lose their jobs (when, for
example, industry moves elsewhere to take advantage of cheaper labor),
are forced to live in substandard housing, are too poor to secure proper
food or health care, are uprooted by road and street improvements, are
left alone in their elderly years. Not everyone can take advantage of the
educational and cultural opportunities of the city; both the lack of money
and the lack of instruction can prevent one's access to the resource of
higher education. The environment is polluted with industrial waste.
There is the omnipresence of dirt, smell, and ugliness. Neighborhoods
are scheduled for deterioration as insurance companies and banks withdraw their support. People grow in oblivion of the person next door. To
be sure, there are sinful structures in the community of the city; there is
disunity at every turn. But there are also grace and the forces of unity
and community. These are our concern here: the thrusts toward greater
community, toward the improvement of community.

Many thinkers today are attempting to improve the effectiveness of
the city. They note that the relatively uncontrolled expansion, characteristic of industrial cities of the last century or so, cannot continue in its
present mode. The expansion has devoured the countryside. It has left
shambles in the center or near the center of the city. It has polluted the
living environment with noise, smell, dirt, and ugliness.

There is the suggestion that cities become more compact, that they
use less of the arable land surrounding the city. Paolo Soleri, for instance,
envisions a city built "on 3-4 square miles in a sea of public grounds and
parks."[56] A centered city would concentrate its living quarters, its industry, its business, its recreational facilities in a restricted area. Everyone would live in the "center" of the city, not far from employment, recreation, cultural events, and educational opportunities. The architecture
of the living quarters, business buildings, and industrial housing would
conform both to the immediate environment and to the needs of the community. There would be an ecological symbiosis between the city community and its physical surrounding. This suggestion, a kind of salvation
by architecture, is idealistic; but it points in the right direction. It is de-

signed to halt the destructive expansion of the city and to center people in a place where fruitful community living is possible.

Another suggestion is that city planning be pursued in terms of the region. Isolated planning on the part of small groups of peoples can result in disorder and neglect of the ecological problems that face the whole area. The small unit such as the neighborhood is important, but it is turned outward in the direction of the whole city or the whole region. The region is built up organically, that is, with concern for a living development of housing, business, etc., on the model of a living organism. The architect Peter Broberg suggests organism as the model of regional development. "The metropolis (the regional conurbation) is in this context regarded as an organic regional body and is called an *urbanism*."[57] "Urbanisms are defined as organically planned regional cities and are to be regarded as members of a new bio-technic species."[58] Just as higher forms of organisms, especially *homo sapiens*, develop a skeleton and make their contact with the surroundings through the organs and muscles of the whole living unit, so also the city develops a living skeleton and comes into contact with the surrounding area through its living quarters, business buildings, etc. As the organism concentrates organs along the vertebrae, so also the region develops in a linear direction by locating necessary industries, communications, businesses, and living quarters along a direct line. A linear direction takes account of the surroundings. Just as a living organism maximizes its interface with the surrounding area through an enveloped skin, through organs of sight and hearing, so also the city—planned in a regional fashion—takes account of the immediate surrounding and is always interacting with the ecological surroundings. Such urbanisms, Broberg holds, must be dispersed throughout the world: "Cutting across political boundaries, the world consists of a number of geographical regions, each with its ecological and cultural background."[59] Global planning is needed "where integration of common interests can occur as well as an equitable division of resources between the different regions."[60]

The city, especially when it is viewed in terms of a region, symbolizes the community of humankind. It manifests ways in which all peoples are one community, one world, one village. The way in which the units of a city act and interact provides a model for the way in which the regional units of the world act and interact. From one standpoint the city-regions of the world are units that work together to form one community of humankind. The units are directed toward each other to solve problems of living on this planet; they depend on each other for their physical and spiritual well-being; they engage in a constant interchange of ideas, talent, and material. The cities of the world are mutually dependent. No city can be entirely independent of the rest of the regions of the earth. The process of interaction, if one is to believe Teilhard de Chardin and others, is becoming increasingly intense and complex. More order and directedness are required on the part of the regions and on the part of structures above the regional-city. There is a world order of city-regions.

The point I wish to make in this section is that the city in its developing complexity and sensitivity can be regarded as a symbol of grace. It can provide an image of what grace is designed to be: a union of people in the service of each other and in the development of their whole selves. God works through the city, and the Scriptures see it as a symbol of the ultimate goal of human striving: living together in the presence of God.

7. The Eschatological Community

The grace of community that overcomes the sin of disunity finds its ultimate and definitive fulfillment in the eschatological community. In a certain sense the fulfillment of the eschatological age is now. Jesus proclaims: "This is the time of fulfillment. The reign of God is at hand! Reform your lives and believe in the gospel" (Mark 1:15). Jesus embodies the reign of God in his person, in his words and deeds. He initiates the final age in which the power of God is manifest in forgiveness of sins and in the gifts of the Holy Spirit: "It shall come to pass in the last days, says God, that I will pour out a portion of my spirit on all mankind" (Acts 2:17, citing Joel 3:1). The Spirit is the integrative force of community; he provides the spiritual energy and the powerful gifts that bring about the unity among peoples of the world.

The eschatological age has arrived but its final shape has not yet appeared. It has been initiated in the Lordship of Jesus Christ, but it will be brought to perfection only in a time to come. It will be brought to perfection by the power of God and by the divine-human forces that are already at work in the world: the forces of the kingdom that believers preach and work to extend; the forces of those who unknowingly cooperate with the presence and call of God to effect the works of justice and peace. The power of God brings to completion the eschatological age, but it is an age that is already in progress through the person of Jesus and through the words and works that his followers continue to perform. The eschatological age will be completed in a time that the Lord chooses, for it is finally God's design and election.

The final shape of the eschatological kingdom is an object of expectation. Christian life is marked by a hope that looks into the future for the completion of a movement already in progress. Christian life is presently a communion in Christ, but it is also an eager expectation of the glorious appearance of the Lord. Christians hope for an outcome of their present experience of Christ, an outcome that will be the ultimate manifestation of the kingdom and the final gathering of God's people. They do not claim to know the time of the kingdom or the details of its final shape, but its expectation enters into a definition of their present belief and hope.

Does the community structure that presently characterizes the fellowship in Christ continue in the eschatological age? Christian tradition is nearly unanimous in its expectation of a heavenly assembly, a city of God: "For here we have no lasting city; we are seeking one which is to come" (Heb 13:14). The author of Hebrews contrasts the earthly Jerusalem with the heavenly; Christian believers need not long for the splendor of the earthly Jerusalem but look forward to the joys of the heavenly. The Book of Revelation records the coming of a new Jerusalem: "Then I saw new heavens and a new earth. The former heavens and the former earth had passed away, and the sea was no longer. I also saw a new Jerusalem, the holy city, coming down out of heaven from God, beautiful as a bride prepared to meet her husband" (Rev 21:1-2). Chapter 21 describes the new Jerusalem with its gathering around the lamb.

The image of the new Jerusalem does not provide a detailed description of the heavenly city. It points to the continuing presence of the heavenly saints in the presence and enjoyment of God. It does not indicate that the present authority and sacramental structures of the Church will continue in the heavenly city. But it does disclose that some kind of assembly of the people in the splendor and enjoyment of God will perdure. The present gathering of people around the person of Jesus will receive a transformation so that the bonds of unity, the modes of coherence, and the manner of communication will be enhanced. More cannot be envisioned.

The eschatological gathering will be centered in God, in the risen Lord, and in their Spirit. The heavenly gathering will bring about an increased experience of God. Traditionally this is called the blessed vision of God (beatific vision), but it is more properly understood as a new experience of God that involves, not just the organ of sight, but all the powers of the human person. It is an experience of togetherness in the presence of God, not an isolated enjoyment of God, each for himself or herself. It is a communitarian enjoyment of God, enhanced precisely because it is communitarian. The present communitarian structure of the recognition and experience of God continues in the eschatological age. The community abides, but in a transformed state.

The communitarian experience of God in Christ is brought to its sharpest focus for us now in the celebration of the Eucharist. The sharing of the bread and wine as the real symbols of the Body and Blood of Christ is a foretaste of the experience of Christ in the time to come. The sharing will become more intense and manifest, but it will continue the mode of communication that is begun in the Eucharist now. "Christ left to his followers a pledge of this hope and food for the journey in the sacrament of faith, in which natural elements, the fruits of man's cultivation, are changed into His glorified Body and Blood, as a supper of brotherly fellowship and a foretaste of the heavenly banquet."[61]

Teilhard de Chardin, whose whole thought sweeps toward the end, speaks of the Omega Point as the ultimate term of the whole process of evolution. The Omega Point is the risen Lord Jesus who comes in glory at the parousia. This thought is evident in the Book of Revelation: "I am the Alpha and the Omega, the First and the Last, the Beginning and the End" (Rev 22:13). The Omega Point is the end toward which the present movement of evolution is oriented. In fact, it is the point from which the present movement receives its essential power of ever increasing complexification and unification. The power of Christ, which is a power of love, reaches back to the very origin of the human species, even back to the beginning of the cosmos, to provide the energy and direction of the whole movement. The whole movement is already set upon the end, which is the whole Christ; Christ, his people, and the world form the end point of the whole process. Teilhard's reflection on the Sacred Heart of Jesus sums up this vision: "Seventh Day, 1st, Friday (December 1, 1939). The Sacred Heart: Instinctively and mysteriously for me, since my infancy: the *synthesis* of Love and Matter, of Person and Energy. From this there has gradually evolved in me the perception of Omega—the universal cohesion in unity."[62]

Teilhard's vision of convergence and unification is communitarian. He does not foresee a disappearance of the individual in the arrival of the end time but rather a maximum personalization and yet a community of God's people gathered about the glorified Christ. "Since everything in the universe, starting from Man, takes place in the personalized being, the ultimate Term of the universal Convergence must also possess (in a supreme degree) the quality of a Person."[63] "There [the heavenly Jerusalem], the original Multitude of bodies and souls—vanquished, but still recognizable and distinct—will be encompassed in a Unity that will make it one single spiritual thing."[64] The disunity of the multitude is overcome in the end time; all are gathered into unity, but it is a unity that preserves distinctness.

The idea that "union differentiates" is one of Teilhard's basic visions.

> What will happen on the day when, in place of the impersonal Humanity put forward by modern social doctrines as the goal of human effort, we recognize the presence of a conscious Center of total convergence? At that time, the individuals caught up in the irresistible current of human totalization will feel themselves strengthened by the very movement which is bringing them closer together. The more they are grouped under a Personal, the more personal they will themselves become. And that effortlessly, by virtue of the properties of love.[65]

Some wonder whether the future kingdom will involve a personal survival. Is it enough to maintain that the reign of God will abide into the future but that individuals will not experience a personal vision of God? J. Cobb speaks of a post-personal future, but he means a transcending of the isolation that persons now experience and the intimate coherence of persons in the future:

> We need now to envision a post-personal future. In such a world there will be a rich interpenetration of each in the other to the intensification and harmonization of the experience of all. This will constitute a new kind of community transcending both collectivities and voluntary associations of autonomous persons. . . . If we can dream of partly transcending our isolated individuality even in this life, then our eschatological vision might share that transcendence and go beyond it. The community for which we hope overcomes isolation without annihilating selfhood.[66]

It is my conviction that some kind of personal survival will continue in the future kingdom. It is, of course, not possible to depict the nature of this survival. The most any of us can do is to extrapolate from our present experience of God in Jesus Christ. The Christian experience of the present moment is personal, that is, it involves a personal relationship to a real man, Jesus Christ, and to a God who is addressed in personal terms. It seems proper to hold, as Christian tradition has held, that this personal dimension of the experience of God will continue into the future.

There is some question about the fate of the physical universe in the eschatological age. Will it be destroyed? Will it remain the same? Or will it be transformed? Certain passages of Scripture seem to indicate that it will be destroyed: "The heavens and the earth will pass away but my words will not pass" (Mt 24:35). Other passages seem to indicate that the universe will be transformed: "Then I saw new heavens and a new earth. The former heavens and the former earth had passed away, and the sea was no longer" (Rev 21:1). The tradition of the Church maintains the glorification of the whole human person—body, soul, and spirit—in the blessed experience of God. One could always hold that at least this much of the present universe is preserved and transformed: the human person composed of flesh and spirit.[67] But it seems reasonable also to hold that the communitarian experience of God will take place in this universe, even a transformed universe, where humans have grown up and to which they have become accustomed. The goodness and value of the universe is viewed as something to be preserved, not to be destroyed in an age to come. And humans will form community and come to experience God in a communitarian fashion, even if in a transformed communitarian fashion.

"Indeed, the whole created world eagerly awaits the revelation of the sons of God. Creation was made subject to futility, not of its own accord but by him who once subjected it; yet not without hope, because the world itself will be freed from its slavery to corruption and share in the glorious freedom of the children of God" (Rom 8:19-21). The physical world shares the marks of human failure (cf. Gen 3:17), and it will also share the future glory of human redemption.

The mystical tradition of Christianity provides many examples of personal, ecstatic union with God. From Saint Paul who encountered the exalted Christ on the road to Damascus, to Saint John of the Cross, Teilhard de Chardin, and untold numbers of people through the centuries, there is a personal experience of God's presence and love which can be called mystical or ecstatic. The literature of the mystics is most often set in terms of the isolated individual. It is the individual who has the indescribable experience of God, who is caught up in the bright light of God (or darkness, to use another image). The mystical experience is not described as communal in the sense that a number of persons experience it at the same time, in the same place, and in the same manner. It should be noted, however, that the mystic is always a member of a community; his or her mystical experience, brief or prolonged, does not make the person withdraw from the community of believers and from the communal worship of the Church. It seems that mysticism is experienced alone, but still there is reference to a community.

It should be noted too that the Christian tradition does not teach a merging of self in the supreme Principle as some Eastern traditions do when they actually mention a union with God. The Christian tradition teaches a unity of consciousness in the mystical experience of God in the world to come; and it also holds that there is a heavenly assembly of those who experience the splendor of God. Thus the mystical tradition of Christianity does not speak of isolation of the spirit but of a community experience of God in the eschatological age.

8. Summary of Chapter 3

If disunity is the symbol of sin, community is the symbol of grace. The community is the place where divisions are overcome, disunity is repaired, isolation is dispelled. The community provides the togetherness of people: their union, fellowship, and concern.

The community is as small as a family or a neighborhood and as large as humankind. But there are graced features of all communities: mutual support, opportunities for growth and love, exchange of goods and services. The community of the city is especially a place of personal and cultural development, a place of harmonious centeredness.

Of necessity, communities share goods and visions, values and services. It is their ideal to be sensitive to the norms of living in a symbiotic relationship with the earth. It is their pride to share the bountiful gifts of the earth.

The community of the Church, fellowship in Christ, is a clear symbol of grace. The Church exists as a gathering of those who adhere to the person, word and work of Christ. It exists to provide humans the effective sacraments of reconciliation, both with God and with one another. It offers a place of meeting the Lord, a place of healing and freedom. In short, it exists to overcome the loneliness of isolation and to effect a communion of persons.

The religious community, in particular the monastic community, supplies a model of the Church. It brings to focus communitarian aspects of the Church, for it gathers in its midst those who symbolize by their relationship to each other the union in Christ that is the goal of all Christian living.

The community, finally, is a symbol of the ultimate conditions of humans, an experience of God in a final age. Togetherness in the Lord now is the symbol of an eschatological assembly in the Lord. Grace is communitarian at the present time and grace will be communitarian in the final convergence, where humans will be gathered together in the presence of the Lord and God will be all in all.

Footnotes

CHAPTER 3

[1]See, e.g., L. Schnore: ". . . I shall regard 'the community' as the localized population which is interdependent on a daily basis, and which carries on a highly generalized series of activities in and through a set of institutions which provides on a day-to-day basis the full range of goods and services necessary for its continuity as a social and economic entity." Ed. N. J. Smelser, *Sociology: An Introduction* (New York: John Wiley and Sons, 1973[2]), p. 75; see also L. Wirth, *On Cities and Social Life* (Chicago: The University of Chicago Press, 1964), p. 166; and T. Parsons, *Societies: Evolutionary and Comparative Perspectives* (Englewood Cliffs, N.J.: Prentice-Hall, 1966), p. 17.

[2]"Community, Society and the State," *The American Benedictine Review*, 28 (1977), p. 80. It is questionable whether Christian theologians would agree that the universal community is the kingdom of heaven on earth; some might be willing to say that it is a limited manifestation of the kingdom.

[3]See Victor Turner's definition of *communitas* in *Dramas, Fields, and Metaphors: Symbolic Action in Human Society* (Ithaca, N.Y.: Cornell University Press, 1974), pp. 201-202.

[4]*The Idea of a Christian Society, Christianity and Culture* (New York: Harcourt, Brace and World, 1968), p. 50.

[5]"Future and Unity," *Hope and the Future of Man*, ed. E. H. Cousins (Philadelphia: Fortress Press, 1972), p. 76.

[6]*The Manual of Discipline. The Dead Sea Scriptures.* In English Translation with Introduction and Notes by Theodor H. Gaster (Garden City, N.Y.: Anchor Books Edition, 1976), p. 44.

[7]"Fellowship, Have, Share, Participate," ed. C. Brown, *The New International Dictionary of New Testament Theology*, Vol. 1 (Grand Rapids, Mich.: Zodervan, 1975), p. 641.

[8]"Was there a core of 'perfecti' in the community (cf. Matt 19:21) of whom a total surrender of goods was demanded (as at Qumran; cf. 1QS 8:20 ff)?" *The Jerome Biblical Commentary*, eds. R. Brown, S.S., J. Fitzmyer, S.J., and R. Murphy, O.Carm. (Englewood Cliffs, N.J.: 1968), 45:32.

[9]Art. 69, *Vatican Council II*, p. 975.

[10]Art. 69, p. 975.

[11]"The Spirit of Earth," *Building the Earth* (New York: Avon Books, 1969), p. 67.

[12]"The Church in the Modern World," *Vatican Council II*, Art. 33, p. 933. See also Teilhard de Chardin: "The true union of loving collaboration, as it grows, brings increased sharing and communion while at the same time those collaborating help each to develop his or her own unique personal traits, talents, and characteristics." Cited in *Proceedings of the Catholic Theological Society of America*, 34 (1979), p. 146.

[13]See Chapter V of Clark M. Eichelberger, *U.N. The First Twenty Years* (New York: Harper & Row, 1965).

[14]*Political and Social Essays*. Collected and edited by D. Stewart and J. Bien (Athens: Ohio University Press, 1974), p. 137.

[15]C. Eichelberger, *U.N. The First Twenty Years*, p. 105.

[16]"A Copernican View of World Cooperation," *The Teilhard Review*, 13 (1978), p. 80.

[17]*Political and Social Essays*, p. 150.

[18]Para. 4. See *Peace and Justice* (St. Paul, Minn.: The North Central Pub. Co., 1979), p. 3.

[19]Kotaro Tanaka: "Briefly, the problem of peace, in the sense of the establishment of a new legal order among conflicting sovereign states, as opposed to appealing to the armed force of each state, is essentially of a legal nature. This problem can be reduced to that of the realization of the rule of law in international society, or more concretely the establishment of world law (or universal law), the creation of an effective world organization and international legislative policy toward peace." *World Crisis and the Catholic* (New York: Sheed and Ward, 1958), p. 134.

[20]"The Church in the Modern World," Art. 88, p. 997.

[21]Part III, B,1. The bishops then quote Pope John XXIII's encyclical letter "Peace on Earth" (137) to the same effect.

[22]*Christianity and Culture*, p. 123.

[23]*Ibid.*, p. 132.

[24]*Ibid.*, p. 136.

[25]So the WCC in Nairobi. See *Breaking Barriers. Nairobi 1975*, ed. D. Paton (London: SPCK, 1976), p. 79.

[26]"The Church in the Modern World," Art. 55, p. 959.

[27]Art. 75, p. 983. See also Pope Paul VI in his encyclical letter "On the Development of Peoples," para. 64-65.

[28]"The Church, moreover, acknowledges the good to be found in the social dynamism of today, particularly towards unity, healthy socialization, and civil and economic cooperation." So Vatican Council II, "The Church in the Modern World," Art. 42, p. 942.

[29]"The Church in the Modern World," Art. 57, p. 962.

[30]"What God is up to: The Ephesian Connection," *Christian Voices on World Order: The Whole Earth Papers*. Vol. 1, no. 10 (East Orange, N.J.: Global Education Associates, 1978), p. 23.

[31]F. Hauck, *Theological Dictionary of the New Testament*, Vol. III (Grand Rapids, Mich.: W. B. Eerdmans, 1965), p. 804.

[32]K. Nickle, *The Collection: A Study in Paul's Strategy* (Naperville, Ill.: A. R. Allenson, 1966), p. 129.

[33]"This togetherness takes many forms. The deep mutuality of understanding and acceptance, made possible by the operation of Christian love in the family circle, is often central. The community of mind and spirit experienced in the *koinonia* of church is absolutely indispensable. And if this in-group togetherness is truly rooted in Christ, then it will find its inevitable and decisive expression in a Christian concern for persons, events, and structures in the whole wide world around." So Arnold Come, *Agents of Reconciliation* (Philadelphia: The Westminster Press, 1964), p. 44.

[34]J. Walgrave, *Person and Society: A Christian View* (Pittsburgh: Duquesne University Press, 1965), p. 131.

[35]Vatican Council II, "The Church in the Modern World," Art. 38, p. 937.

[37]D. Bonhoeffer, *Life Together* (New York: Harper & Row, 1954), p. 20.

[37]D. Bonhoeffer, *Life Together*, p. 22.

[38]Cf. all the forms of sin that we discussed in Chapter 1.

[39]Victor Turner views the pilgrimage as a social process and a liminal phenomenon. The pilgrimage journey and the pilgrimage center are ways of experiencing God, of seeking healing, and of moving from sin to grace. "I am suggesting that the social mode appropriate to all pilgrimages represents a mutually energizing compromise between structure and communitas; in theological language, a forgiveness of sins, where differences are accepted or tolerated rather than aggravated into grounds of aggressive opposition." *Dramas, Fields, and Metaphors: Symbolic Action in Human Society* (Ithaca, N.Y.: Cornell University Press, 1974), p. 208.

[40]*Grace in Experience and Theology* (Minneapolis, Minn.: Augsburg Pub. House, 1977), p. 201.

[41]P. Tillich, *Systematic Theology*, Vol. II, p. 166.

[42]J. Jeremias, *New Testament Theology. The Proclamation of Jesus* (New York: C. Scribner's Sons, 1971), p. 177.

[43]See J. Theisen, *The Ultimate Church and the Promise of Salvation* (Collegeville, Minn.: Saint John's University Press, 1976), Chap. 2.

[44]B. Häring, *Sin in the Secular Age* (Garden City, N.Y.: Doubleday, 1974), p. 112.

[45]J. Walgrave, *Person and Society*, p. 127.

[46]Vatican Council II, "The Church in the Modern World," Art. 31, p. 931.

[47]With minor alterations this section has appeared as "Community as the Shape of Christian Salvation," in *The Continuing Quest for God. Monastic Spirituality in Tradition and Transition*, ed. William Skudlarek, O.S.B. (Collegeville, Minn.: The Liturgical Press, 1982), pp. 1-8.

[48]This discussion of the paradigmatic character of the monastery will be limited to Western monasticism, and generally to Benedictine monasticism. The limitation does not imply that there are no symbolic features of human community in Eastern monasticism (e.g., in Buddhism). Western Christian monasticism is selected as an example because I am more acquainted with its structures and goals.

[49]*RB 1980. The Rule of St. Benedict* (Collegeville, Minn.: The Liturgical Press, 1981).

[50]Cf. the 1978 Jonestown disaster.

[51]See *The Sayings of the Desert Fathers*, transl. by Benedicta Ward (London: A. R. Mowbray & Co., 1975), p. 123.

[52]See Hannah Arendt, *The Human Condition* (Garden City, N.Y.: Doubleday Anchor Books, 1959), pp. 25-26.

[53]See Harvey Cox, *The Secular City* (New York: The Macmillan Co., 1965).

[54]"The Church in the Modern World," Art. 43, p. 943.

[55]*Ibid.*

[56]*The Bridge between Matter and Spirit is Matter Becoming Spirit: the Arcology of Paolo Soleri* (Garden City, N.Y.: Anchor Books, 1973), p. 49.

[57]*Regional Urbanisms: The Evolution of a New Macrospecies* (London: The Teilhard Centre, 1978). See *The Teilhard Review*, 13 (1978), p. 5.

[58]*Ibid.*, p. 6.

[59]*Ibid.*, p. 13.

[60]*Ibid.*, p. 61.

[61]Vatican Council II, "The Church in the Modern World," Art. 38, p. 937.

[62]Unpublished Retreat Notes 1939-1943. Cited in R. Faricy, "The Heart of Jesus in the Eschatology of Teilhard," *The Teilhard Review*, 13 (1978), p. 84.

[63]"The Spirit of Earth," *Building the Earth*, p. 71.

[64]*Writings in Time of War*, pp. 175-176.

[65]"Human Energy," *Building the Earth and the Psychological Conditions of Human Unification* (New York: Avon Books, 1965), p. 85. Cf. *The Phenomenon of Man* (New York: Harper Torchbook, 1961), p. 263. See also R. C. Zaehner, *Concordant Discord* (Oxford: Clarendon Press, 1970), p. 408.

[66]"What is the Future? A Process Perspective," ed. E. Cousins *Hope and the Future of Man*, pp. 11-12.

[67]"If we can dream of partly transcending our isolated individuality even in this life, then our eschatological vision might share that transcendence and go beyond it. The community for which we hope overcomes isolation without annihiliating selfhood." J. Cobb, *Ibid.*, p. 12.

Select Bibliography

Bourgeois, Patrick L. *Extension of Ricoeur's Hermeneutic*. The Hague: Martinus Nijhoff, 1975.

Connor, James L., S.J. "Original Sin: Contemporary Approaches," *Theological Studies*, 29 (1968), pp. 215-240.

Eliot, T.S. *Christianity and Culture. The Idea of a Christian Society and Notes Toward the Definition of Culture*. New York: Harcourt, Brace & World, 1968.

Fromm, Erich. *The Anatomy of Human Destructiveness*. New York: Holt, Rinehart and Winston, 1973.

Guilluy, Paul (ed.). *La Culpabilité Fondamentale: Péché Originel et Anthropologie Moderne*. Gembloux: Duculot, 1975.

Haag, Herbert. "The Original Sin Discussion, 1966-1971," *Journal of Ecumenical Studies*, 10 (1973), pp. 259-289.

Hegel, G. W. F. *Phenomenology of the Spirit*. Transl. by A. V. Miller with Analysis of the Text and Foreword by J. N. Findlay. Oxford: Clarendon Press, 1977.

Ihde, Don. *Hermeneutic Phenomenology: The Philosophy of Paul Ricoeur*. Evanston, Ill.: Northwestern University Press, 1971.

Lasch, Christopher. *The Culture of Narcissism: American Life in an Age of Diminishing Expectations*. New York: W. W. Norton & Co., 1979.

Lowe, Walter James. *Mystery and the Unconscious: A Study in the Thought of Paul Ricoeur*. Metuchen, N.J.: Scarecrow, 1977.

———. "The Coherence of Paul Ricoeur," *The Journal of Religion*, 61 (1981), pp. 384-402.

Mac Isaac, Sharon. *Freud and Original Sin*. Paramus, N.J.: Paulist Press, 1974.

McDermott, Brian O., S.J. "The Theology of Original Sin: Recent Developments," *Theological Studies*, 38 (1977), pp. 478-512.

Mesters, Carlos. *Eden: Golden Age or Goad to Action?* Maryknoll, N.Y.: Orbis Books, 1974.

Niebuhr, Reinhold. *Nature and Destiny of Man: A Christian Interpretation*. New York: C. Scribner's Sons, 1941-43.

———. *The Children of Light and the Children of Darkness: A Vindication of Democracy and a Critique of Its Traditional Defense*. New York: C. Scribner's Sons, 1944.

Paton, David M. (ed.) *Breaking Barriers: Nairobi 1975*. London: SPCK, 1976.

Plaskow, Judith. *Sex, Sin, and Grace: Women's Experience in the Theologies of Reinhold Niebuhr and Paul Tillich*. Washington, D.C.: University Press of America, 1980.

Rasmussen, David M. *Symbol and Interpretation*. The Hague: Martinus Nijhoff, 1974.

Reagan, Charles E. (ed.) *Studies in the Philosophy of Paul Ricoeur*. Athens: Ohio University Press, 1979.

Richard, Jean, M.S.C. "Introduction à la doctrine du symbolisme religieux chez Paul Tillich," *Laval Théologique Philosophique*, 29 (1973), pp. 23-56.

———. "Symbolisme et analogie chez Paul Tillich." *Laval Théologique Philosophique*, 32 (1976), pp. 43-74. 33 (1977), pp. 39-60; pp. 183-202.

Ricoeur, Paul. *Fallible Man: Philosophy of the Will*. Chicago: H. Regnery Co., 1965.

———. *Freedom and Nature: The Voluntary and the Involuntary*. Evanston, Ill.: Northwestern University Press, 1966.

———. *The Symbolism of Evil*. New York: Beacon Press, 1969.

———. "Philosophy of Will and Action." *Phenomenology of Will and Action*. Ed. by Erwin W. Straus and Richard M. Griffith. Pittsburgh: Duquesne University Press, 1967, pp. 7-33, pp. 41-43, pp. 57-60.

———. "The Problem of the Double-Sense as Hermeneutic Problem and as Semantic Problem." *Myths and Symbols: Studies in Honor of Mircea Eliade*. Eds. by Joseph M.

Kitagawa and Charles H. Long. Chicago: University of Chicago Press, 1969, pp. 63-79.
_____ . "The Problem of the Will and Philosophical Discourse." *Patterns of the Life-World: Essays in Honor of John Wild.* Eds. by James M. Edie, Francis H. Parker and Calvin O. Schrag. Evanston, Ill.: Northwestern University Press, 1970, pp. 273-289.
_____ . *Freud and Philosophy: An Essay on Interpretation.* New Haven, Conn.: Yale University Press, 1970.
_____ . *The Conflict of Interpretations: Essays in Hermeneutics.* Evanston, Ill.: Northwestern University Press, 1974.
_____ . *Interpretation Theory: Discourse and the Surplus of Meaning.* Fort Worth: Texas Christian University Press, 1976.
Rowe, William L. *Religious Symbols and God: A Philosophical Study of Tillich's Theology.* Chicago: University of Chicago Press, 1968.
Scheffczyk, Leo. *Urstand, Fall und Erbsünde: von der Schrift bis Augustinus.* Freiburg: Herder, 1981.
Schoonenberg, Piet, S.J. *Man and Sin.* Notre Dame, Ind.: University of Notre Dame Press, 1965.
Segundo, Juan Luis, S.J. *Evolution and Guilt.* Maryknoll, N.Y.: Orbis, 1974.
Soleri, Paolo. *Arcology: The City in the Image of Man.* Cambridge, Ma.: M.I.T. Press, 1969.
_____ . *The Bridge between Matter and Spirit is Matter Becoming Spirit: the Arcology of Paolo Soleri.* Garden City, N.Y.: Anchor Books, 1973.
Stuhlmueller, Carroll, C.P. "Repentance for Original Sin and Reconciliation in Christ," *Communio,* 1 (1974), pp. 20-46.
Taylor, Charles. *Hegel.* Cambridge: Cambridge University Press, 1975.
Teilhard de Chardin, Pierre, S.J. *Writings in Time of War.* New York: Harper & Row, 1968.
_____ . *Christianity and Evolution.* New York: Harcourt Brace Jovanovich, 1969.
_____ . *The Divine Milieu.* New York: Harper, 1960.
Tillich, Paul. "The Religious Symbol," *The Journal of Liberal Religion,* 2 (1940), pp. 13-33.
_____ . *Systematic Theology.* 3 Vol. Chicago: University of Chicago Press, 1951-63.
_____ . "Theology and Symbolism" *Religious Symbolism.* Ed. F. Ernest Johnson. New York: Harper & Brothers, 1955, pp. 107-116.
_____ . "Existential Analyses and Religious Symbols." *Contemporary Problems in Religion.* Ed. Harold A. Basilius. Detroit: Wayne University Press, 1956, pp. 35-55.
_____ . *Dynamics of Faith.* New York: Harper & Row, 1957.
_____ . "The Meaning and Justification of Religious Symbols." *Religious Experience and Truth. A Symposium.* Ed. Sidney Hook. New York: New York University Press, 1961, pp. 3-11.
Tracy, David. "St. Thomas and the Religious Dimension of Experience: The Doctrine of Sin," *Proceedings of the American Catholic Philosophical Association,* 48 (1974), pp. 166-176.
Vandervelde, George. *Original Sin. Two Major Trends in Contemporary Roman Catholic Reinterpretation.* Amsterdam: Rodopi, 1975.
Vanneste, Alfred. "Le dogme de l'Immaculée Conception et l'evolution actuelle de la théologie du péché originel," *Ephemerides Mariologicae,* 23 (1973), pp. 77-93.
_____ . *The Dogma of Original Sin.* Brussels: Nauwelaerts, 1975.
_____ . "Où en est le problème du péché originel?" *Ephemerides Theologicae Lovanienses,* 52 (1976), pp. 143-161.
Watté, Pierre. *Structures philosophique du péché originel: S. Augustin, S. Thomas, Kant.* Gembloux: Duculot, 1974.